Machine Embroidered
Quilting and Appliqué

Simple Steps for Revolutionary Results

Eileen Roche

kp

KRAUSE PUBLICATIONS
CINCINNATI, OHIO

Machine Embroidered Quilting and Appliqué: Simple Steps for Revolutionary
Results. Copyright © 2011 by Eileen Roche and Nancy Zieman. Manufactured in
China. All rights reserved. No part of this book may be reproduced in any form or
by any electronic or mechanical means including information storage and retrieval
systems without permission in writing from the publisher, except by a reviewer
who may quote brief passages in a review. Published by Krause Publications, a
division of F+W Media, Inc., 4700 East Galbraith Road, Cincinnati, Ohio, 45236.
(800) 289-0963. First Edition.

 www.fwmedia.com

15 14 13 12 11 5 4 3 2 1

DISTRIBUTED IN CANADA BY FRASER DIRECT
100 Armstrong Avenue
Georgetown, ON, Canada L7G 5S4
Tel: (905) 877-4411

DISTRIBUTED IN THE U.K. AND EUROPE BY F&W MEDIA INTERNATIONAL
Brunel House, Newton Abbot, Devon, TQ12 4PU, England
Tel: (+44) 1626 323200, Fax: (+44) 1626 323319
Email: enquiries@fwmedia.com

DISTRIBUTED IN AUSTRALIA BY CAPRICORN LINK
P.O. Box 704, S. Windsor NSW, 2756 Australia
Tel: (02) 4577-3555

Library of Congress Cataloging in Publication Data
Roche, Eileen (Eileen Ward)
  Machine embroidered quilting and appliqué : simple steps for revolutionary
results / Eileen Roche. -- 1st ed.
     p. cm.
  Includes index.
  ISBN-13: 978-1-4402-1398-4 (alk. paper)
  1. Embroidery, Machine--Patterns. 2. Appliqué--Patterns. 3. Quilting--Patterns.
I. Title.
  TT772.R623 2011
  746.44'5--dc22
                        2010044474

Edited by Jennifer Claydon

Designed by Steven Peters

Production coordinated by Greg Nock

Photography by Eileen Roche and Al Parrish

Styling by Lauren Emmerling

ABOUT THE AUTHOR

Eileen Roche is considered an expert
in the home machine embroidery
industry. Founding editor of *Designs
in Machine Embroidery* magazine,
Eileen has invented many products
that embroiderers depend on to
make machine embroidery more
successful and enjoyable.

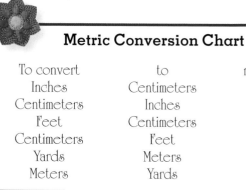

Metric Conversion Chart

To convert	to	multiply by
Inches	Centimeters	2.54
Centimeters	Inches	0.4
Feet	Centimeters	30.5
Centimeters	Feet	0.03
Yards	Meters	0.9
Meters	Yards	1.1

DEDICATION

This book—and the hundreds of hours of work that kept my head down consumed in stitching and writing—is dedicated to two friends, Helen Gardner and Scott Moore. Whenever I struggled with a deadline, I humbly thought of them and their gallant charge toward a healthy lifestyle.

ACKNOWLEDGMENTS

Even though I created every project in this book, from the digitizing to the selecting of fabrics to the stitching of each block, I couldn't have done it without the backup of my team at *Designs in Machine Embroidery.* It's because they are so proficient at their jobs that I had the freedom to focus on such a large-scale project.

Denise Holguin runs the magazine efficiently and punctually even when I've dropped my responsibilities. She keeps track of every project, photo shoot, email blast, advertiser, sample . . . oh, for heaven's sake, I can't list all of her responsibilities! You wouldn't believe them if I told you. Just know that she is the power behind the magazine. I am grateful for her hours—no, years—of dedication and her inspirational input into our business model.

Sam Solomon, Creative Director, makes the mag and all of our products look beautiful. And often he does it with little guidance, keeping everything moving in a timely fashion. Not so easy to do when you're waiting for important files from others—OK, from me!

The newest addition to the staff, Amanda Griffin, is our Web Czar. Yes, she has the coolest title on staff, but boy, does she earn it. She's even capable of translating foreign Internet lingo into terms I can grasp! No easy task there.

Lorraine Allen is our main customer service rep; if you call the office, there's a good chance you'll talk to Lorraine. A passionate embroiderer, Lorraine handles the embroidery questions that many readers expect us to answer. Like how to import designs into their digitizing software. Not really our area of responsibility, but Lorraine often tackles the difficult questions!

Stephanie Stubbs has grown up at the magazine—literally. She started with us as a teenager and has blossomed into our Accounting/Purchasing Customer Service representative. She keeps track of orders, shipments, dealers and so on, all with a smile on her face.

Of course, no business is worth its while unless its product is getting out the door. Bryant Royal rules the warehouse—nothing comes in or out without his blessing. We can always count on Bryant, a native Texan, to share his warm Texas humor along with his artistic skills (you oughta see what he can draw!) with each of us. It's a joy to work side by side with him.

As you can see, there are many different areas of responsibilities, and they all have to "talk" to each other. By "talk," I mean link computer-wise. The man behind that is Roy Garland. Amanda might be our czar, but Roy is our wiz. We'd still be writing with pencils if Roy weren't catapulting us into the future!

There are a few other people who made this book possible. Nancy Zieman's nudging helped me agree to accept this responsibility, and taping with her is always a joy. My business partner, Gary Gardner's support of these techniques is, well, cool. He has been a great mentor, cheerleader and partner.

Finally, Pete Kutsopias, my sweetheart, tolerated my unavailability on weekends and evenings as I "worked my second job." Not a quilter or embroiderer, he bravely gave his opinion on fabric selections and the like when asked. Which is like answering the trap question of "Do these pants make me look fat?"

I know it's a cliché, but the wind beneath my wings is my children. My daughter, Janelle, helped with the final finishing of *Lady Liberty*. Every time I look at that quilt, I see her nimble hands pressing the blocks and adding the binding. A lovely memory. My son, Ted, on the other hand, would fly through the sewing room, occasionally acknowledging a massive amount of work in progress on the design wall. If he stopped, I knew I was onto a winning project. He's a delightful barometer!

You wouldn't be holding this book in your hands if it wasn't for my publisher, F+W Media. Many thanks to my editor, Jenni Claydon, for keeping me on schedule and improving my "voice." The gorgeous design of Steven Peters was brought to life by Al Parrish and Lauren Emmerling while Greg Nock made sure everything happened on schedule. Thank you for creating a beautiful, educational book.

Table of Contents

Introduction

What is Revolutionary about Machine Embroidered Quilting and Appliqué?

Machine Embroidered Quilting and Appliqué is about traditional quilting techniques transformed by an embroidery machine. The whole process of traditional quilting is turned upside-out. Instead of piecing first, then quilting, these revolutionized quilt blocks are quilted, appliquéd, removed from the hoop, then pieced. These steps eliminate the tiresome minute cutting and piecing of traditional quilting techniques.

These quilt blocks are created through a brand-new technique that involves the sequencing of thread colors, layering of raw edge appliqués and trimming after the block is removed from the hoop. Because all blocks are created by a digital file, all blocks will be identical in size—something I've always had difficulty achieving with a rotary cutter and ruler.

No stabilizer is required because you'll hoop the backing, batting and the quilt top fabric together. You'll learn how to stitch evenly spaced embroidery designs or connect designs for a seamless linking of quilting or appliqué. There are three methods for continuous embroidery—explore the one that works best for you and your machine.

All of the blocks are pieced with a simple, reversible piecing technique with front and back sashing. The sashing strips become a decorative element in the quilt and can be sized, pieced or split for a variety of looks. Most of the projects feature quilter-friendly ½" seam allowances, which lead to piecing success for all levels of quilters.

This is a revolutionary, "out of the box" approach to quilting, and you will have to leave your comfort zone to explore these techniques. But trust me, if you have a desire to create—and finish!—beautiful quilted projects in a reasonable amount of time, then these techniques are worth a try. What I love about this new technique is that my quilts are now perfectly square, unlike most of my past projects, and I can actually finish what would normally be daunting, if not impossible, quilt projects.

Give these new techniques and projects a try—I'm sure your quilting will be revolutionized!

CHAPTER 1

What You'll Need

The beauty of machine embroidered quilting and appliqué is that you will use what you probably already have on hand for quilting or machine embroidery. You'll most likely have the basic embroidery tools: an embroidery machine with a minimum 5" × 7" sewing field, standard embroidery hoops, threads and needles. Consider making your life easier by investing in some tools that simplify the embroidery process such as magnetic hoops, an Angle Finder, target rulers and target stickers.

You'll also need a computer to transfer the embroidery designs from the included disk onto your embroidery machine. Embroidery editing software is helpful if you like to view each design in detail before commencing on a project. I also recommend printing templates of the designs—this will give you a printed image of the design and help with placement if you are using standard embroidery hoops.

Basic quilting tools will also be needed, and tackling machine embroidered quilts gives you a new excuse to shop for fabrics. If your stash is full of busy-print or large-scale print fabrics, then it might be time for a shopping spree. Since the appliqué fabrics are the stars in a machine-embroidered quilt, it is best to make sure they stand out from the base fabric either in color, value or print. All blocks fit in a 5" × 7" hoop, so large-scale prints are lost on the small canvases. Evaluate your stash after reviewing the guidelines in this chapter.

Throughout the book you'll also find some new terms. Take the time to familiarize yourself with the words used to describe these revolutionary techniques so you'll understand them when you come across them in the instructions.

Technology and Terminology

DESIGNS

The embroidery designs on the disk included with this book have been digitized specifically for raw edge appliqué. They are not traditional embroidery designs—there are no fill stitches or satin-stitched edges. The designs feature two stitch types: run and bean. The bean stitch, a triple run of thread, is used in all appliqué tackdowns to securely hold the appliqué to the base fabric. Some of the designs have placement guides that illustrate where to place the appliqué fabric, but some do not because it will be obvious where the appliqué fabric should be placed—over the large blank hole in the quilting stitches. An in-depth look at all the designs is featured on the disk.

VOCABULARY

These new techniques require some new, unique terms. Here are a few words I'll use throughout the book that you should become familiar with:

Alignment marks: stitched arrows used to connect or link two or more designs; alignment marks are the first color stitched in a design and can be removed after all embroidery is complete

Base fabric: the fabric directly on top of the batting; use interchangeably with *quilt top*

Bean stitch: a triple stitch created when the needle penetrates the fabric at point A and travels to point B, then back to point A and back to point B before advancing to point C to lay the next stitch

Frame: (noun) embroidery hoop; (verb) to center an area of fabric within the embroidery hoop's sewing field

Machine Embroidered Quilting and Appliqué: traditional quilting techniques transformed by an embroidery machine

Placement guide: a stitched outline that shows where to place the appliqué fabric; the placement guide will be hidden by the appliqué fabric.

Quilt cracker: quilt top and batting

Quilt sandwich: quilt top, batting and backing

Quilt top: the fabric directly on top of the batting; use interchangeably with *base fabric*

RST: right sides together

Tackdown: straight running stitches that hold down the edge of an appliqué (usually in the form of a bean stitch)

Tie-off: tiny repetitive stitches that secure the bobbin and needle threads

WOF: width of fabric, from selvage to selvage

WST: wrong sides together

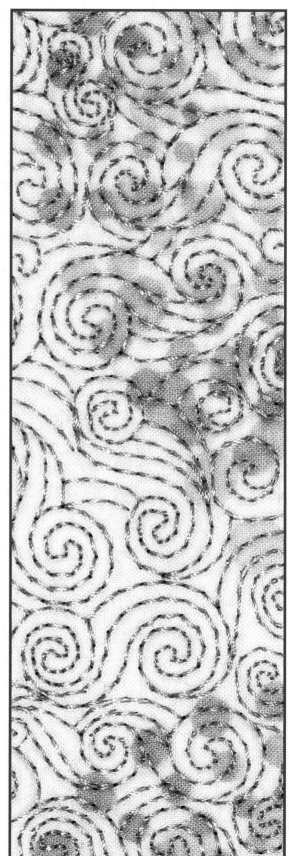

Materials

APPLIQUÉ FABRICS

The appliqué fabrics in these projects are the stars of the show. Even though these techniques use machine embroidery, the focus of the appliqué is the fabric, not the embroidery stitches. This technique gives the appearance of tediously applied appliqué or intricate piecing. The success of these machine embroidered appliqué projects depends on the visibility of the appliqué. Contrast in color or value is what will make the appliqué designs pop.

Make an Impact with Color

I use a color wheel to help select fabrics. A color wheel is divided into three primary colors: yellow, magenta and cyan. There are many different ways to group colors to create visual interest.

Complementary colors are colors that are opposite each other on the color wheel. These are tried-and-true combinations. To find a complementary appliqué fabric, place your base fabric on a color wheel and move your eye across the wheel: There's your appliqué fabric! This method, used in the *Lady Liberty Quilt* on page 100, works beautifully and guarantees eye-catching results.

Analogous colors sit next to each other on the color wheel. They blend beautifully together and help move from one color family to the next. The pink, orange and yellow colors of the *Sewing Notions Caddy* on page 86 are a good example of analogous colors.

Monochromatic colors are shades and tints derived from the same color family. You can make a monochromatic color scheme work successfully in this technique. The cream, tan and brown colors of *My Favorite Bag* on page 78 display a successful monochromatic color scheme.

Make an Impact with Value

Although color is powerful, so is value. The value of a color is the amount of white or black that's been added to its true color. When white is added to a pure color, a tint is created. When black is added to a pure color, a shade is created. If you have trouble remembering these terms, think how anything in the shade is darker (and duller) than anything in

the sun. Anything that is lit is brighter—or tinted. When gray is added to a pure color, shade or tint, the result is a tone.

Value is what separates one fabric from another and moves the eye across the quilted surface. The value of one fabric depends on the values of the other fabrics in the quilt. A medium blue will appear dark when placed on a pale blue. Conversely, a medium blue will appear light when placed on a midnight blue. It is the difference in value that makes appliqués stand out from their surroundings. Appliqué fabrics that separate from the base fabric give the most impact. Consider using a value finder—a red or green piece of acrylic that eliminates the color in a fabric—to look at your fabrics. You'll see only the fabric's value.

Always audition appliqué fabrics on the base fabric. Dark base fabrics might show through lighter appliqué fabrics. If your base fabric shows through your appliqué fabric, you can still use this combination, but you might want to fuse an interfacing to the wrong side of the appliqué fabric to make it opaque.

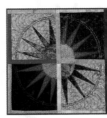 

Complementary colors   *Analogous colors*   *Monochromatic colors*

11

QUILT TOP FABRICS

In my opinion, solid fabrics or low-contrast prints work best for the projects in this book. Because I'm an embroiderer first and a quilter second, I learned early on that printed fabrics compete with embroidery stitches. So I always seek out plain or color-washed fabrics. I do like some interest in the fabric, like hand-dyed cottons, low-contrast batiks and tone-on-tone prints.

With these techniques, cotton fabrics will give you the same results as they would in a traditional quilting project. Consider exploring silks and silk/cotton blends for a more upscale and textured finish. The sheen of these fabrics adds more visual texture to the quilting stitches.

A home-dec weight cotton fabric also works great for the quilted bags. The dense weave of these fabrics and their heavier weight add strength and structure to bags. Consider using home-dec weight cottons for projects that will get a lot of wear and tear.

The fabrics used in this book are 100% cotton, 45" wide and were not prewashed prior to use. If the final use of the project will include laundering, then prewash your fabrics. If not, then don't bother.

BACKING

The back of an embroidered quilt will not be the same as the back of a traditional quilt. If you view award-winning, traditionally made quilts from the back, you will discover many are just as beautiful from the back as they are from the front. If this is the look you are after, consider purchasing a long-arm quilting machine. That's the tool to get the professional, "Which side is the front?" look.

The techniques in this book are fast, easy and manageable on a single-needle embroidery machine—a machine you already own. So what's the matter with the back of these projects? The thread tension is not balanced, and you'll spot many tie-offs. The tension on an embroidery machine is set to pull the top thread, the decorative thread, to the wrong side. This provides a beautiful finish on the right side of an embroidery design, but leaves a rather unsightly scene on the back. Some machines allow the user to override the tension and deliver a balanced stitch. If this is your desire, refer to your machine manual to reset the tension.

However, you may have to reset it every time you load a new design. This is where I often mess up—I forget to change the setting for a new design. I wind up with half the blocks with balanced tension and the other half not! After encountering this dilemma numerous times, I gave up and switched to busy prints for the back. These prints camouflage the inevitable embroidery machine tie-offs and unbalanced stitches. It's also a great use for those novelty fabrics that don't coordinate well with embroidery. I tend to purchase black-and-white prints in large quantities, ten yards at a time, from the bargain table. If I run out of a print during a quilt, I'll substitute another black-and-white print. Since I stay with black-and-white prints, all the blocks coordinate.

BATTING

Cotton batting and cotton/poly blend batting produce luxurious results with these projects. Fusible batting also works well, especially when you are using large embroidery hoops. Experiment with different brands to find your favorite and follow the manufacturer's directions for fusing the batting to the fabrics. Low- to medium-loft batting works best in embroidered quilts since bulky batting can be difficult to secure in an embroidery hoop.

All of the projects in this book were made with Warm & Natural or Warm & White batting (both by the Warm Company). These battings have no need for pre-washing because there is less than 3% shrinkage. I love the soft hand, durable strength and needle-punched texture of these battings.

THREAD

There are so many choices of thread—rayon versus polyester, 30wt. versus 40wt. All of the designs on the included disk were tested with 40wt. rayon and polyester thread. A higher sheen was achieved with the polyester thread and the colorfastness of polyester is often desirable. However, thread fiber is a personal choice. Experiment with your stash and go with what works for you. Since the designs do not have fill stitches, a 30wt. thread could theoretically be used for bolder, more pronounced stitches. I suggest testing any design on scrap fabric before using a different weight thread.

Tools

EMBROIDERY TEMPLATES AND TARGET STICKERS

Templates tell you many things, including the actual size of the embroidery, the location of the center of the design and the orientation of the design. A template provides a visual image of the finished design before you take a stitch. To make your own templates, open the design in embroidery editing software and print from there. Seeing the actual size of the embroidery design is helpful when planning embroidery. Often you'll need to know where one design ends and the other begins when connecting two or more embroidery designs.

Knowing the orientation of a design is crucial when planning and stitching embroidery. The orientation of the design is determined by what part of the design will stitch at the top of the hoop. We often take the orientation of a design for granted, especially in lettering. For instance, we can be confident that the letter M will stitch in a portrait orientation and always be the proper finished monogram for Mary and not Wilma. In many other designs, such as the Fleur de LisF1 design on the *Trapunto Table Runner* on page 64, the orientation is not what is normally expected. In order to fit the large design in a 5" × 7" hoop, the design was rotated and saved in a landscape orientation. If you don't use a template to plan the embroidery layout, there's a good chance the design will stitch in an unintended direction.

Knowing the location of the center of the design is important because it is where the needle will be positioned when the design is selected on the embroidery machine. If your template is not centered on the hooped fabric, you can move the hoop to position the needle over the center of the template. A template is a helpful tool for navigating in the hoop.

Target stickers can be used in conjunction with templates for positioning a design. Once you have created your embroidery layout with printed templates, use target stickers to designate the center of each template. This eliminates the cumbersome task of hooping with pieces of paper taped or pinned to the fabric. Just slide a target sticker under the template, aligning the crosshairs on the template and sticker. Remove the template and hoop the fabric. Target stickers can also be used to designate the outer edges of a previously stitched design when linking a second design (see page 25).

Without the template, one might assume this was the probable orientation of the Fleur de LisF1 design when embroidering, but it actually stitches out a different way.

This template includes the number of stitches in the design, the number of thread colors used, the actual size of the design and the actual orientation of the design.

ANGLE FINDER

If your fabric is crooked in the hoop, you can still stitch it straight if your machine features 1-degree or 5-degree rotation. You can use an Angle Finder to discover exactly how much rotation is required to stitch an embroidery design as planned. With the combination of templates, target stickers and the Angle Finder, every design can be stitched perfectly straight.

First, position a template on the quilt sandwich in the desired location. Hoop the quilt sandwich (Figure 1). Don't worry about hooping perfectly square.

Next, slide a target sticker under the template (Figure 2). Center the Angle Finder on the target sticker with the 0 degree facing toward the upper edge of the hoop (Figure 3).

While keeping the Angle Finder's black crosshair squared with the hoop's outer edges, rotate the dial on the Angle Finder so the red arrowhead is aligned with the target sticker (Figure 4).

Note the rotation degree that the red arrow designates. Make sure both arrows (target sticker and red crosshair) are facing in the same direction. Rotate the design on the screen using the rotation keys until you reach the number you found using the Angle Finder. Embroider the design.

Angle Finder, Figure 1

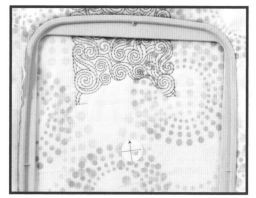

Angle Finder, Figure 2

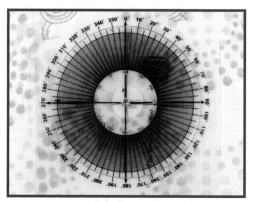

Angle Finder, Figure 3

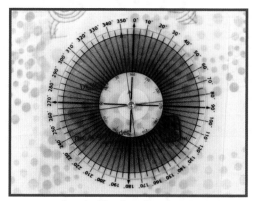

Angle Finder, Figure 4

NOTES FROM NANCY

Eileen and I were taping a *Sewing With Nancy* series several years ago when I said, "I sure wish there was a tool that could measure the degree of angles." Instantly, I could see the proverbial wheels turn in Eileen's head. Within a few months, this great tool was born. I know that you'll use it as much as I do!

Target Rulers

Target rulers can be used to locate the center of a quilt block, hoop or any other area. You can also use one to measure the distance between embroidery designs or to find out if you are square in the hoop.

To find the center of a quilt block, place the target ruler on the block so the outer dimensions of the block sit on the ruler's equal increments. For example, for a 6" block, the edge of the block should hit the 3" point on each arm of the ruler to find the center (Figure 1).

When embroidering numerous blocks on a quilt strip, you can use a target ruler to measure the distance between each block (Figure 2). For the projects in this book, blocks will be separated 1"–1½" for seam allowances.

Often it's important to check if the fabric is square in the hoop. Place a target ruler on the hoop, aligning one straight line on the ruler with a straight line on the hooped fabric (a pressed crease, marked line, painter's tape, template or seam). The arms of the target ruler should hit the hoop at equal marks (Figure 3).

Painter's Tape

Apply a length of painter's tape just outside the edge of an embroidery area as an alignment guide. It is a helpful visual aid when stitching continuous quilting and appliqué designs (Figure 1).

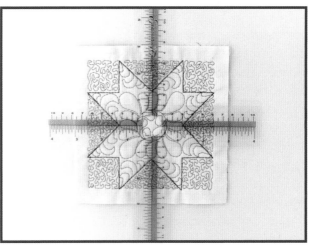

Target Rulers, Figure 1

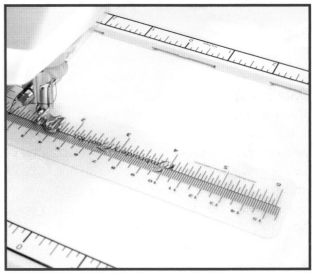

Target Rulers, Figure 2

Painter's Tape, Figure 1

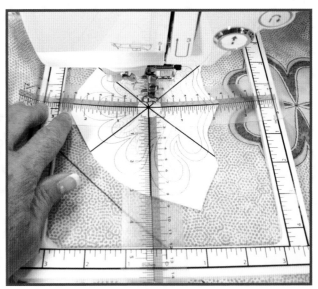

Target Rulers, Figure 3

HOOPS

Standard embroidery hoops consist of an inner and outer ring; the fabric is held between the two rings. Standard hoops provide the strongest tension on fabric for the embroidery process. Once secured in the hoop, the fabric cannot be tugged or pulled without distorting the fibers.

Magnetic hoops secure fabric with a flat metal bottom frame and a flat acrylic or plastic frame on top. Magnets attract the two frames with a firm hold. Because the fabric is flat, it can be pulled, tugged and adjusted right in the frame without any fabric distortion. Magnetic hoops are ideal for stitching on quilt sandwiches and making minute fabric adjustments under the needle. Magnetic hoops come in two styles, one that rests on the inner frame of a standard embroidery hoop and one that is a stand-alone hoop. Two of my favorite magnetic hoops are the Magna-Hoop Jumbo and the Snap-Hoop.

Magna-Hoop Jumbo sits on the rim of a standard embroidery hoop's inner ring. It firmly holds a quilt sandwich when all eight magnets are in the corresponding slots. Fabric adjustments can be made by removing some of the magnets, moving the fabric and placing the magnets back in position.

Snap-Hoop is a flat, magnetic, stand-alone hoop. It firmly grips all three layers of a quilt sandwich and enables an embroiderer to make minute adjustments to design placement right at the machine.

To hoop a quilt sandwich in a magnetic hoop, hold one end of the fabric beyond the frame, then pull or smooth the quilt sandwich with the opposite hand. Release the fabric, align the top and bottom frames and stitch the design.

When repositioning the fabric for the next design, just lift the top frame, slide the fabric into position and place the top frame back in position.

QUILTER'S TOOLS

A cutting mat, rotary cutter and 24" quilter's ruler are a must for any quilting project. The quilter's ruler should be translucent with ¼" markings. You'll use these tools to trim and square the quilt blocks and strips.

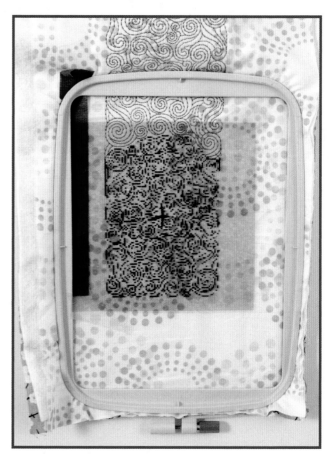

Quilt sandwich in Magna-Hoop Jumbo

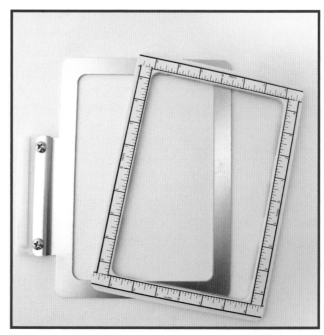

A Snap-Hoop

16

Machines

Many different embroidery machines are available today with prices ranging from $300 to over $10,000. Why such a disparity in price? The answer is in the features. An embroidery machine can be a stand-alone unit or a combination of sewing and embroidery. It can have a computer built in or can be powered by a separate desktop or laptop computer. A home embroidery machine will have one needle and can possibly accommodate a number of hoop sizes.

Where do you start when purchasing an embroidery machine? Hopefully, right in your hometown. Embroidery machines can be highly technical—a helpful, knowledgeable sewing machine dealer that is geographically close to you is worth its weight in gold. Don't necessarily shop by brand; instead, shop by dealer. Visit several local dealers and select the one that offers education, on-site repairs and is a place you enjoy visiting. Then test drive! Decide what features are important to you and then sit down at several models in your price range. Take the machine through some common tasks, such as selecting an embroidery design and making a few on-screen edits. If you feel comfortable with the screen, the layout, the keys, etc., it could be the machine for you!

There are many features that entice embroiderers. Here are a few of my favorites.

Media: I love an embroidery machine that accepts a USB memory stick because it transfers the designs right from my computer to the machine.

Hoop size: A 5" × 7" sewing field is the smallest field that I would consider when purchasing an embroidery machine. A larger sewing field (7" × 10" or larger) is helpful, but not mandatory, so skimp here if your budget is tight.

On-screen editing: A highly visible LCD screen makes selecting and editing designs a breeze. I like seeing the design on the screen in full color.

Perimeter tracing: This feature travels around the outermost edges of a design without taking a stitch. It's helpful when checking accuracy of placement.

Hoop movement: Because I do most of my design editing at my computer, the most important feature for me at the machine is the ability to position the needle over any spot in the hoop. I say "position the needle" because the needle does not move—the hoop moves. I want to see the needle positioned directly over a target sticker or template before I take a stitch.

One-degree rotation: I couldn't live without the ability to rotate in tiny increments.

Mirror image: This cuts down on computer design and transfer time.

There are also a few luxurious features that one may get accustomed to quickly. They are automatic threading systems, automatic thread trimmers, low bobbin indicators and the ability to read multiple formats. Of course, the number-one feature is the stitch quality. Your embroidery machine should present you with beautiful embroidery, so look for it first when shopping for a new machine.

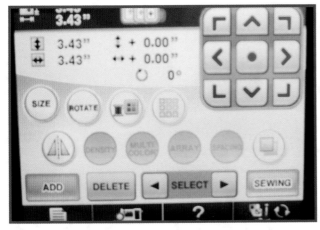

Editing on an LCD screen.

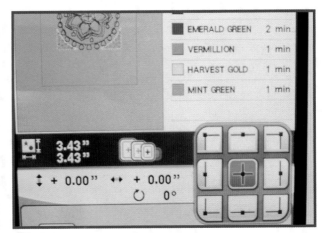

Rotating a design on an LCD screen.

CHAPTER 2

Simple Steps for Machine Embroidered Quilting and Appliqué

This chapter reveals the secrets to the revolutionary techniques in this book. Take the time to read through the whole chapter to grasp this innovative process before beginning a project. I've turned the traditional method of quilting (cutting, piecing, appliquéing and quilting) on its head. The projects in this book are made in reverse: quilting, appliquéing, cutting and piecing. I break down all the steps into simple, manageable sections. You'll be amazed how easily it all comes together.

Of course, every quilt's look depends on the fabrics you choose to include. Start with a quilt sandwich of backing, batting and quilt top fabric. Then select appliqué fabrics to add punch to the design. Use color and value to make the blocks pop. You'll be impressed how time-consuming traditional blocks such as *Ohio Star*, *Lady Liberty* and *New York Beauty* come alive in a few minutes with the selection of contrasting fabrics.

Some sections of the projects serve as accents and do not include appliqué fabrics. They provide an area of rest for the eye and don't compete with the other blocks. You'll learn three different methods to stitch continuous quilt strips: target stickers, stitched alignment marks and templates. Try all three methods to find the one that gives you the most success. When you master that method, move on to continuous appliqué strips. Continuous appliqué is my favorite technique because it appears to be very complicated (but it isn't!). The pattern on the continuous strips can travel the length of the border without interruption. Consider this technique when you want to showcase a special fabric.

19

Preparing Materials

MAKING THE QUILT SANDWICH

Unlike traditional quilt piecing, embroidered quilt blocks start with pieces of fabric that are larger than the finished size of the block. The large blocks or strips are hooped, and all embroideries and appliqués are applied to the blocks. After all embellishment is complete, the blocks or strips are cut to the finished size (plus seam allowances).

The trade-off of this super-simple technique is an ample supply of fabric scraps. If care is taken in the initial cutting, block placement and trimming, much of the waste can be used for sashings or other projects.

In order to make the most economical use of fabric, I recommend ripping a strip that is 11" × the width of fabric (WOF) for projects that use multiple blocks. An 11" × WOF strip of 44"-wide fabric yields at least six blocks in a 5" × 7" embroidery hoop. By adding 5" to the width of a 6" finished block (this includes ½" seam allowances on all sides), you can cut a 2" strip from each side of the block to use for sashing. (The extra 1" is included to alleviate the pressure of hooping perfectly square.)

To make the quilt sandwich, place the backing fabric right side down on a pressing surface and press it. Smooth a matching strip of batting over the backing fabric and press it. Place the quilt top fabric, right side up, on the batting and press once again. Flip the quilt sandwich over and smooth the back. Set this aside and repeat these steps to make the number of quilt sandwiches required for the project.

If you are using a large hoop (6" × 10" or larger), consider fusing the layers together with temporary spray adhesive. If you choose to do this step, work in a large, ventilated area and protect your work surface with a sheet of vinyl, or work outdoors. Lay the backing and quilt top strips wrong sides up on the protected surface. Generously spray the fabrics with temporary adhesive. Place the batting strip over the backing fabric. Work at one end of the strip and smooth the batting to the tacky surface. Continue to work toward the opposite end. Once all wrinkles or bubbles are removed, place the quilt top strip, wrong side down, on the batting, and smooth it as well.

A quilt sandwich strip with several appliqués applied.

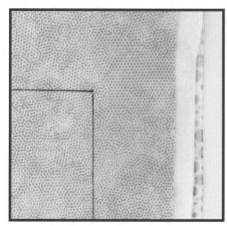

A quilt sandwich with backing right side down, batting, and quilt top fabric right side up.

NOTES FROM NANCY

Another alternative to using spray adhesive is to fuse-baste the layers! Cut ½" squares of paper-backed fusible web, such as Wonder Under. Fuse squares at 3" intervals to the wrong side of both the top and backing layers. After removing the paper backing, layer the quilt sandwich and press. The fusible squares baste the layers together.

PREPARING APPLIQUÉ FABRICS

Because most trimming is done after the quilt blocks or strips are removed from the hoop, appliqué fabrics do not need to be cut into precise shapes or sizes. To cut the appropriate amount of appliqué fabric, determine how many blocks or appliqués you will create with a specific appliqué fabric. Cut a strip of fabric about 1" wider than the appliqué width (6" is a safe measurement as no block is wider than 5" in this collection). Cut the length of the strip to measure 6" × the number of appliqués you will make (for example, for six appliqués, cut a strip at least 6" × 36").

To get the most durability out of the appliqués, consider the use of the project and the amount of decorative stitching that is applied to each appliqué. All appliqués on lap quilts, pillows and tote bags should be prepared for a final step of heat bonding because normal wear and tear of these items could otherwise cause the appliqués to come loose.

To prepare appliqué fabrics for heat bonding, apply paper-backed fusible web to the wrong side of the strip. Follow the manufacturer's directions for applying the fusible web to the wrong side of the appliqué fabric. Remove the protective paper and set aside. If you add fusible web, do not press the quilt blocks before trimming the appliqués. Permanent fusing to the quilt top is done after the trimming process. If you iron the quilt block before you trim the appliqué, you will fuse the entire piece of appliqué fabric to the quilt top fabric and you will not be able to trim it.

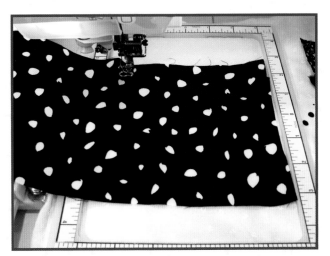

A strip of appliqué fabric laid over a quilt sandwich in the hoop.

Making Quilted and Appliquéd Components

QUILTED BLOCKS

Quilted blocks are used as accent blocks in a variety of quilt layouts. They do not have any appliqué fabric. Each quilted block is made of a quilt sandwich: batting, backing and the quilt top. It is then quilted using an embroidery machine. Because most quilted blocks in this collection are decorative feather patterns, use a contrasting thread to bring attention to the details.

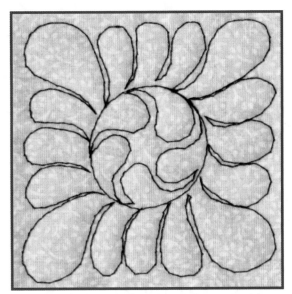

A quilted block from the Ohio Star Quilt *on page 94.*

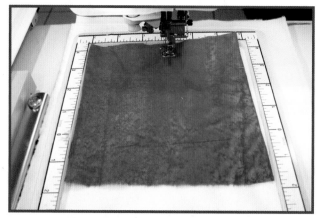

Single-Color Appliqué, Figure 1

APPLIQUÉD BLOCKS

Appliquéd blocks feature quilting as well as appliqués in one or more colors. Each appliquéd block will need a quilt sandwich plus appliqué fabric(s). To begin, cut the quilt sandwich to fit your hoop. (All designs in this collection fit in a standard 5" × 7" hoop.) To determine the size of your quilt sandwich for an individual block, lay the hoop on a flat surface and measure the outside perimeter of the hoop. Add 3" to this length and width, and cut the quilt sandwich to these dimensions. If you are making multiple blocks, refer to Making the Quilt Sandwich on page 20. Hoop the quilt sandwich. Make sure all layers are smooth and taut in the hoop.

Single-Color Appliqué

Stitch color 1, the quilting stitches, on the base fabric (Figure 1). Here, it is a stipple.

Place the appliqué fabric over the base fabric after stitching color 1. Smooth the appliqué fabric over the hooped quilt sandwich (Figure 2).

Sew color 2, the appliqué tackdown (Figure 3).

Sew the next color(s), the quilting stitches, on the appliqué (Figure 4).

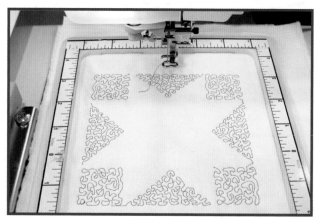

Single-Color Appliqué, Figure 2

Single-Color Appliqué, Figure 3

Single-Color Appliqué, Figure 4

22

Remove the quilt sandwich from the hoop. Carefully trim the appliqué. Place the blade of the scissors close to the stitched outline and slice away the fabric (Figure 5). Snip into the inner corners to remove the fabric. Take small snips to avoid cutting the thread at the inner corner (Figure 6).

Two-Color Appliqué

The process of making appliquéd blocks changes slightly when two appliqué fabrics are used. When selecting fabric for two-color appliqué blocks, both appliqué fabrics should contrast with the base fabric.

The process begins like a Single-Color Appliqué: First, stitch color 1, the quilting, on the base fabric. After completing color 1, lay the first appliqué fabric on the block. Stitch the next color(s), the tackdown of the first appliqué. Then, stitch the next color(s), the quilting, on the appliqué (Figure 1).

Remove the hoop from the machine and carefully trim the fabric away from the area where the second appliqué will be placed (Figure 2).

Reattach the hoop to the machine. Lay the appliqué fabric for the second appliqué over the opening in the block. Make sure the appliqué fabric extends ½" into the seam allowance beyond the block dimensions (Figure 3).

Stitch the next color(s), the tackdown and quilting stitches, on the second appliqué.

Remove the quilt sandwich from the hoop. Carefully trim the appliqué as you would for a Single-Color Appliqué (see above).

Single-Color Appliqué, Figure 5

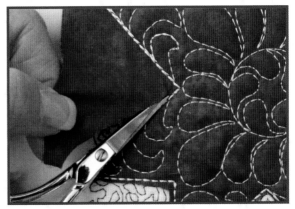

Single-Color Appliqué, Figure 6

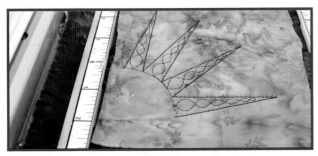

Two-Color Appliqué, Figure 1

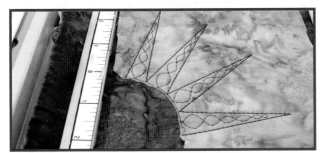

Two-Color Appliqué, Figure 2

Two-Color Appliqué, Figure 3

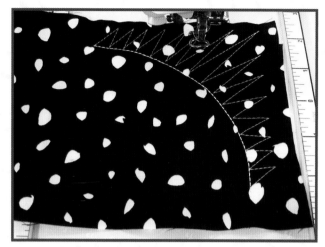

Multi-Color Appliqué, Figure 1

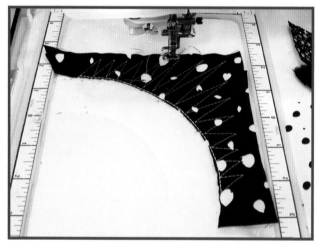

Multi-Color Appliqué, Figure 2

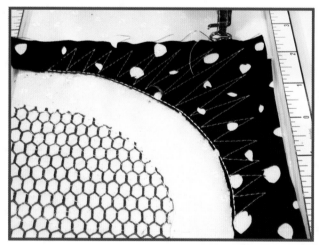

Multi-Color Appliqué, Figure 3

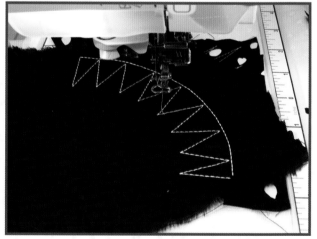

Multi-Color Appliqué, Figure 4

Multi-Color Appliqué

For appliquéd blocks with more than two colors, the process for Two-Color Appliqué is repeated for each additional color: sew appliqué 1, trim for appliqué 2, sew appliqué 2, trim for appliqué 3, etc. Begin by stitching color 1 on the base fabric. Place the appliqué fabric over the area for the first appliqué. Stitch the color(s) used to tackdown and quilt the first appliqué (Figure 1).

Without removing the hoop from the machine, trim the fabric away from the area where the second appliqué will be applied (Figure 2).

Place the second appliqué fabric over the area on the base fabric where the second appliqué will be stitched. Stitch the color(s) used to tackdown and quilt the second appliqué. Without removing the hoop from the machine, trim the second appliqué fabric away from the area where the third appliqué will be applied (Figure 3).

Place the third appliqué fabric on the base fabric and stitch the color(s) that will tackdown and quilt the third appliqué (Figure 4). Repeat sewing and trimming until all appliqués are applied.

Remove the quilt sandwich from the hoop and carefully finish trimming the appliqué fabrics as you would for a Single-Color Appliqué (see page 23).

CONTINUOUS QUILTED STRIPS

A quilted area with no appliqué can serve as an accent to add texture to the overall surface, gives the eye a place to rest and lets the appliquéd sections be the stars. Use these when you want to expand the finished project but don't want to add another focal point. There are two methods for continuous quilting.

Target Stickers

Make a quilt sandwich strip of quilt top fabric, batting and backing. Hoop the quilt sandwich at the top left portion of the strip. Stitch a quilting design. When the design is complete, use your machine's perimeter trace feature to position the needle at the bottom left corner of the design. Place a target sticker directly under the needle. Move the needle to the bottom right corner of the design and place another target sticker directly under the needle (Figure 1). Carefully lift the top frame of the hoop and slide the fabric up without dislodging the target stickers. Use the trace feature to position the needle at what is now the top left corner of the design. Place the needle directly over the left target sticker. Move the needle to what is now the top right corner and place it directly over the right target sticker. Use the flywheel to manually drop the needle to verify the position (Figure 2).

The needle should pierce the target sticker in the center of each crosshair. If it doesn't, use one of the following methods to position the needle: you can use the jog keys to move the hoop, you can reposition the fabric by gently tugging on it, or you can lift the hoop's top frame and move the fabric or rehoop.

Once everything is properly aligned, remove the target stickers and embroider the next design.

Stitched Alignment Marks

Continuous quilting can also be achieved by connecting two embroidery designs. Alignment stitches have been added to these designs to make them easy to match up (Figure 3). For designs with alignment stitches, stitch the first design including the alignment marks, then slide the fabric up to frame the next area. Place the needle at the top left corner. Advance to stitch 1 of the second design; if you've placed everything correctly, the needle should connect with the stitched alignment mark. If not, adjust the fabric or use the jog keys to move the design. Continue to advance through the alignment mark, stitch by stitch, to make sure the horizontal lines match and the vertical lines connect at the corners.

Continuous Quilted Strips, Figure 1

Continuous Quilted Strips, Figure 2

Continuous Quilted Strips, Figure 3

When Eileen demonstrated the stitch alignment marks to me, my jaw literally dropped. This feature is truly amazing. You'll see it demonstrated on the DVD — seeing is believing!

NOTES FROM NANCY

25

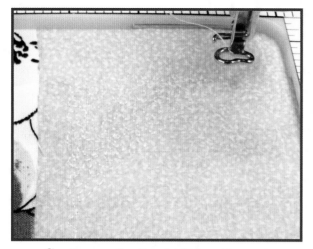

Continuous Appliquéd Strips, Figure 1
This series of photos shows two continuous appliquéd strips, one completed (left) and one in progress (right).

Continuous Appliquéd Strips, Figure 2

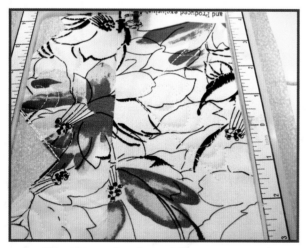

Continuous Appliquéd Strips, Figure 3

CONTINUOUS APPLIQUÉD STRIPS

The Continuous Appliqué technique gives you the ability to create long borders or strips regardless of the limits of your hoop. It looks complicated but is very easy to achieve.

Make a quilt sandwich wide enough to fit in the hoop and as long as the desired border length plus 5". Consider making a wider quilt sandwich to accommodate two or more borders on the same quilt sandwich side by side (spaced at least two seam allowances apart).

Cut a strip of appliqué fabric for each border (the width of the appliqué strip will depend on the width of the appliqué on the strip).

Hoop the top left portion of the quilt sandwich. Stitch color 1, the quilting, on the base fabric (Figure 1).

Place the appliqué strip over the design area. Make sure the width of the strip spans the entire stitched area (Figure 2).

Stitch the appliqué tackdown and the decorative stitching on the appliqué (Figure 3).

Lift the unstitched portion of the strip of appliqué fabric back over the design (Figure 4).

Use your machine's perimeter trace feature to position the needle at the bottom left corner of the design. Place a target sticker directly under the needle. Move the needle to the bottom right corner and place a target sticker directly under the needle (Figure 5).

Carefully lift the top frame of the hoop and slide the fabric up to the unstitched area under the already-stitched area. Don't dislodge the target stickers while moving the fabric. Keep the appliqué strip folded away from the embroidery field. Use the trace feature to position the needle at what is now the top left corner of the design. Place the needle directly over the target sticker. Move the needle to the now top right corner and place it directly over target sticker. Use the flywheel to manually drop the needle (Figure 6).

The needle should pierce the target sticker in the center of the cross hair. If it doesn't, use one of the following methods to position the needle: you can use the jog keys to move the hoop, you can reposition the fabric by gently tugging on it, or you can lift the hoop's top frame and move the fabric or rehoop.

Remove the target stickers and smooth the appliqué fabric into position. Stitch the next design. Continue until the border has been filled.

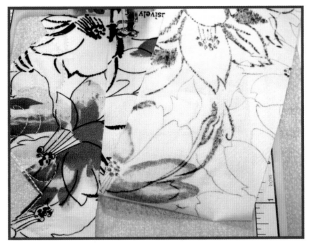

Continuous Appliquéd Strips, Figure 4

Continuous Appliquéd Strips, Figure 5

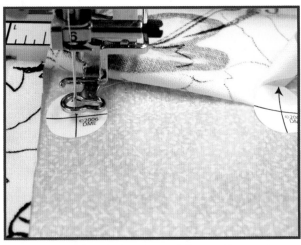

Continuous Appliquéd Strips, Figure 6

CHAPTER 3

Special Effects

Just like in traditional quilting, special effects can really enhance an appliqué fabric or background in the projects in this book. In this chapter we'll explore four techniques to add interest with texture and paint.

Trapunto can be incorporated into many appliqué designs. The key to success here is the layering of the batting. It's important to keep the batting fibers invisible while adding loft to the appliqué. Learn the trick of hiding the batting on page 30.

When working with large blocks, it's tempting to piece the background to add more interest; learn how to keep the background fabrics in the background but give viewers an opportunity to explore the surface a bit more on page 30.

By the very nature of their crafts, quilters and embroiderers love texture. Layering fabrics; stitching swirls, dots and grids; and manipulating fabrics add texture to already luscious fabrics. Incorporate appliqué fabrics with texture already built in, such as wool felt, suede or fleece, into your projects. Or try your hand at texturing plain cotton fabrics with a shrinking stabilizer. It's magical—and happens right under your iron!

Dabbling in other mediums can open your eyes to many possibilities. Learn the effects of pastel paint sticks, brushed on fabric paint and sprayed on fabric paint by experimenting with one design. Stitch repeats of a design on the same fabric to review the results with each method. Get familiar with the techniques, then branch out from there. Who knows where your designs will take you!

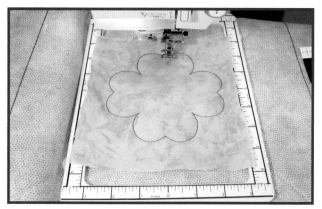

Trapunto, Figure 1

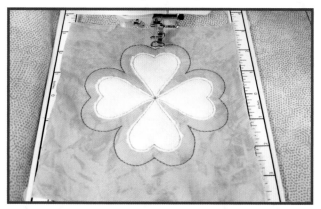

Trapunto, Figure 2

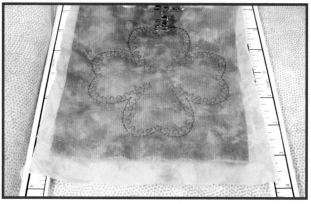

Trapunto, Figure 3

Trapunto

Give a basic appliqué design a lift by adding an extra layer of batting to a portion of the design. This method conceals the fuzzy edge of the batting under the appliqué piece.

First, position the needle over the target sticker crosshair that marks the center of the design. Place a square of appliqué fabric in the center of the hoop. Stitch color 1, the tackdown of the large appliqué (Figure 1).

After completing color 1, place a square of batting over the outline. Stitch color 2, the tackdown of the trapunto batting. Remove the hoop from the machine after stitching color 2. Trim the batting close to the stitched outline (Figure 2).

Place the next appliqué fabric over the large outline and reattach the hoop to the machine. Stitch color 3, the tackdown of the second appliqué. Stitch color 4 as well, the decorative stitching inside the large appliqué (Figure 3).

If the design calls for additional appliqués and stitching, continue until the design is complete. Remove the fabric from the hoop and trim the excess appliqué fabrics.

Pieced Base Fabric

You can add interest to the base of any of the blocks in this book by piecing fabrics together to form the quilt top fabric prior to making the quilt sandwich. Keep in mind that the appliqué will still be the star of the quilt, so keep all base fabrics in the same value. Otherwise, it will be very difficult to select appliqué fabrics that stand out from all of the pieced fabrics. To create a pieced base fabric, piece the fabrics with ¼" seam allowances. Don't restrict the fabrics to equal widths and lengths—play with different proportions to get the look you want. Press the seam allowances to one side. Make the quilt sandwich. Audition appliqué fabrics on the pieced top to find the perfect combination.

Pieced Base Fabric (left)
The base fabric on this block from Basket of Blooms (see page 116) features four fabrics with the same value. The lighter value appliqué fabrics pop from this dark base.

Textured Appliqué

There are two ways to add texture to a machine embroidered quilt block: use textured fabrics such as felt, suede or fleece for the appliqué, or texturize a plain fabric.

TEXTURED FABRIC

Felt is ideal for elevating an ordinary appliqué design. Hoop the quilt sandwich as normal. Stitch the first colors on the base fabric.

Place a piece of felt over the open area and stitch the tackdown. Skip the decorative stitches inside the appliqué; they will only flatten the lofty felt (Figure 1). Voilà, instant lift!

TEXTURIZING FABRIC

Texture Magic is a steam-activated shrinking fabric that is perfect for texturizing appliqué fabrics. Hoop a piece of Texture Magic along with the appliqué fabric. Select a continuous design like Grid oneLineF1 or Diamond GridF2. Stitch the design with monofilament thread in the needle and regular bobbin thread in the bobbin.

Remove the fabric from the hoop and place it with the appliqué fabric face up on a pressing surface. Set the iron for the highest steam setting and burst the steam over the fabric. Do not touch the iron to the fabric. Continue to add bursts of steam and watch the fabric shrivel (Figure 1).

Hoop the quilt sandwich as normal. Stitch the first colors on the base fabric, then place the shrunken fabric over the outline. Stitch any outline and tackdown stitches, but skip decorative fill stitches (Figure 2). Trim the appliqué fabric close to the stitched outline to finish (Figure 3).

Textured Fabric, Figure 1
This coaster features a felt appliqué.

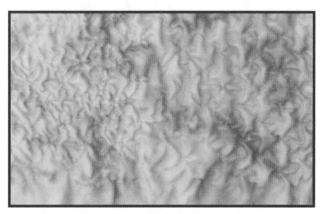

Texturizing Fabric, Figure 1
This appliqué fabric has been stitched and treated with Texture Magic. Grid oneLineF1 is on the left, and Diamond GridF2 is on the right. The closer together the stitches are, the more drastic the results.

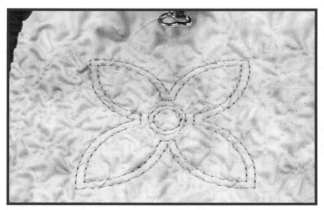

Texturizing Fabric, Figure 2

Texturizing Fabric, Figure 3
This coaster features a Texture Magic appliqué.

Painted Appliqué

I explored three different products for adding color to appliqué sections without adding appliqué fabric. They are pastel paint sticks, brushed on fabric paint and sprayed on fabric paint. I enjoyed each process and was impressed by the variety of looks that could be created without using fabric. I used a tone-on-tone print for the base fabric, which added another dimension to some of the embellished coasters. Stitch the coaster design from *Raggedy Edge Coasters* on page 44 to experiment with these techniques (do not stitch color 5, the stipple inside of the flower).

Pastel Paint Sticks

Let's start with a simple colorway. Stitch a coaster using white fabric and black thread. Select a dark green pastel (or dark color of your choice) and color the petals. Lighten the dark shade with a bright shade (Figure 1).

Fill in the flower center with cherry red or your choice of color (Figure 2).

You can also use this method to produce more complex coloring. Begin by stitching a coaster using white fabric and light gray thread. Select four pastels and start coloring between the stitched lines. Switch to a different color between each set of stitched lines (Figure 3).

Use a light pink (or a light color of your choice) on the petals and give it some life with a soft yellow or other contrasting color. Brushing a new color right on top of another color forms a blended hue (Figure 4).

Pastel Paint Sticks, Figure 1
The petal in the upper left has only the dark green pastel applied, while the rest have a layer of bright green over the dark green, giving the design depth.

Pastel Paint Sticks, Figure 2
This finished coaster looks like Christmas, doesn't it?

NOTES FROM NANCY

Who would have ever thought that we'd be using oil pastels to enhance embroidering? I have found the best assortment of colors available at art supply stores. Remember to purchase oil pastels, not chalk (non-oil) pastels.

Pastel Paint Sticks, Figure 3

Pastel Paint Sticks, Figure 4
The upper petals only have the pink pastel applied while the bottom petals have a layer of yellow.

Select a darker tone for the edges of the petals (Figure 5).

BRUSHED ON FABRIC PAINT

For this technique I used Jacquard Dye-Na-Flow. I was a bit out of my element with these paints, but I love the bold, clear colors. This technique lets the tone-on-tone print shine through, adding even more interest to the striking color combination.

To try this technique, stitch a coaster using white fabric and black thread. Sparingly apply the paint to a dry brush and stroke in the open areas (Figure 1). If you want to fill in the small spaces between the stitched lines, use a narrow, pointy brush for more control. Let the paint dry and heat set it with a household iron.

SPRAYED ON FABRIC PAINT

This technique is a bit unpredictable, so practice if you're going for a certain look.

Begin by stitching a coaster using white fabric and light gray thread. Place strips of ¼"-wide tape on the coaster, spacing the strips ½" apart and extending the strips beyond the coaster edges. Start in the middle and work your way out to the corner.

It's best to spray the paint outdoors, so prepare the coaster indoors, then take it out to spray the paint over the surface. Spray the entire coaster with paint. Hold the bottle about 10"–12" away from the fabric and work with quick shots of paint to avoid blotting (Figure 1).

Let the fabric dry, peel the tape off the coaster and set the paint with an iron (Figure 2).

Pastel Paint Sticks, Figure 5

Brushed on Fabric Paint, Figure 1

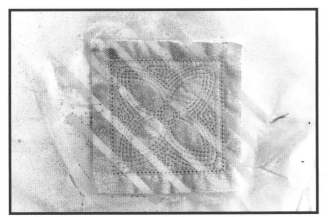

Sprayed on Fabric Paint, Figure 1

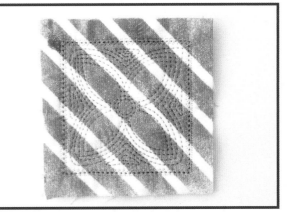

Sprayed on Fabric Paint, Figure 2

CHAPTER 4

Assembling and Finishing Projects

So how do you put it all together? Reversible piecing is the answer. All blocks are pieced into units; units are joined into rows; and rows are made into quilts. Front and back sashing is added in one sweep of the needle. A little ingenious pressing and voila! The quilt is finished, back and front, with no visible seam allowances. Reversible piecing is so versatile you can add cornerstones and pieced sashing with it as well.

Take the time to pin the blocks to the sashing when venturing into pieced sashing and you'll be pleased with the results. I've learned a pin or two can save lots of ripping later! Get creative by adding multiple fabrics to your sashing to really ramp up the design of your quilt. Remember, you're the master here; I'm just showing you some techniques to help you.

Once pieced, it's time to bind the quilt. Because I always seem to be running out of time, I was thrilled when I learned this quick binding method—fusible web to the rescue! Just fuse, slice, fold, press and done. Oh, I love that! Of course, traditional binding methods look beautiful too. You can finish off the edges of your quilt however you wish.

After all that hard work, don't forget the label. You'll find five embroidery designs for labels on the included disk. Add your message with lettering software or write it on the finished label with a permanent marker. Fuse the label onto the back of the quilt, then hand-sew around the edges to permanently attach it. The last step is to enjoy your beautiful creation!

Assembling Units

REVERSIBLE PIECING

Using reversible piecing you can create small, manageable quilted sections and then piece the sections into larger units. Units are pieced to other units to form the finished quilt. Reversible piecing adds sashing to the front and back of the quilted sections simultaneously. To cut the sashing for reversible piecing, use the following formula: double the finished width of the front and back sashing to find the sashing's cut width. The seam allowances are half of the sashing's finished width. For instance, in the *Ohio Star Quilt* (see page 94) a 1" finished-width sashing requires a 2" cut width using ½" seam allowances for piecing. For the *Lady Liberty Quilt* (see page 100), the sashing has a ½" finished width and requires a 1" cut sashing and a ¼" seam allowance.

Piecing Blocks into Units and Rows

Trim all blocks and borders with the recommended seam allowance, here ½" (Figure 1). To do this, place the ½" mark of a quilter's ruler on the edge of the embroidery and trim off the excess. Do this on all four sides of each block.

To piece one block to another, place the front sashing, RST, on the right seam allowance of the first block (Figure 2). Place the back sashing, RST, on the back of the block. Pin through all layers and sew with the appropriate seam allowance for the sashing size—here, ½" (Figure 3). Press the front sashing open (Figure 4).

I like the idea of ½" seam allowances. Unfortunately, not all machines have that guideline marked on the throat plate. For a quick ½" seam allowance, measure ½" from the needle. Remove the brown backing sheet from the back of a pad of sticky notes and apply the entire pad to your machine with the binding side facing the needle. Presto, an instant seam guide!

Piecing Blocks into Units and Rows, Figure 1

Piecing Blocks into Units and Rows, Figure 2

Piecing Blocks into Units and Rows, Figure 3

Piecing Blocks into Units and Rows, Figure 4

Place the left side of the second block RST with the front sashing. Sew with a ½" seam allowance (Figure 5). Press open the second block.

Flip the blocks over—notice how the raw edges meet in the middle of the sashing (Figure 6). Press the back sashing over the seam allowances. Fold the seam allowance (here, ½") under on the remaining long edge (Figure 7).

Pin the back sashing down from the front—I do this with the back of the blocks facing up, and place my hand and pin on the front. This way I can see if the pins catch the folded edge of the sashing.

Stitch in the ditch on the right side of the quilt. Trim the sashing ends even with the edges of the blocks (Figure 8).

Repeat these steps to add additional blocks to complete a row of blocks. Do not add sashing to the ends of the row. Piece all of the rows in this manner. Set aside the rows or display them on a design wall in the proper order.

Piecing Rows Together

Once all of the rows are assembled, they are pieced together using reversible piecing. The horizontal sashing strips between rows can be as simple as a single strip of fabric for the front and back of the quilt, or the sashings can be pieced in a variety of ways.

For a single-fabric sashing between rows, measure the length of the rows. Cut front and back sashing strips to go between the rows. These sashing strips should be the same width as the ones between the blocks, and the length should be equal to the length of the row.

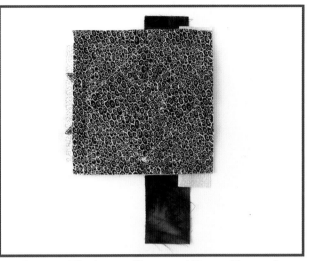

Piecing Blocks into Units and Rows, Figure 5

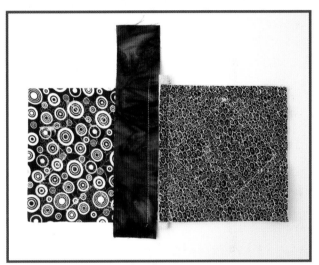

Piecing Blocks into Units and Rows, Figure 6

Piecing Blocks into Units and Rows, Figure 7

Piecing Blocks into Units and Rows, Figure 8

37

You may choose to use pieced sashing on the front of the quilt. One type of pieced sashing is sashing with cornerstones, which is used in the *Ohio Star Quilt* (see page 94). Sashing with cornerstones is made up of solid pieces of sashing between the blocks with a cornerstone where the sashing strips meet (Figure 1). For sashing with cornerstones, cut the front sashing strips as wide as the strips between blocks and as long as the width of one block, plus seam allowances. For the *Ohio Star Quilt*, these measurements are 2" × 7", or: 2" (sashing strip width) × [6" (block size) + 1" (two ½" seam allowances) = 7"]. Cut the cornerstones into squares that match up to the sashing strips—here, 2" × 2". Using ½" seam allowances, sew the sashing strips and cornerstones into a continuous strip as long as the length of the row (Figure 2). Make the number of horizontal sashing strips required for your project.

Another type of pieced sashing is segmented sashing. Instead of connecting to just one block, segmented sashing spans across a block and a vertical sashing strip (Figure 3). Segmented sashings are used in the *Lady Liberty Quilt* (see page 100). To create segmented sashing strips, cut the front sashing strips as wide as the strips between blocks and as long as the width of one block, plus one vertical sashing strip and the appropriate seam allowance. For the *Lady Liberty Quilt*, these measurements are 1" × 6", or: 1" (sashing strip width) × [5" (block size) + ½" (horizontal sashing width) + ½" (two ¼" seam allowances) = 6"]. Join the sashing strips together with the appropriate seam allowance—here, ¼" (Figure 4). Make the number of horizontal sashing strips required for your project.

Piecing Rows Together, Figure 1

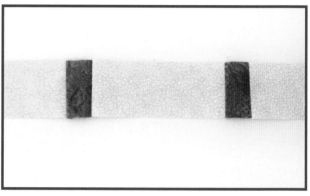

Piecing Rows Together, Figure 2

Piecing Rows Together, Figure 3

Piecing Rows Together, Figure 4

NOTES FROM **NANCY**

Take the lead from Eileen; sashing strips can be different colors of fabric! Untraditional uses of color create visual interest.

To assemble the rows with sashing strips, lay the first front and back sashing strips RST with the bottom edge of Row 1 of the quilt. If you use a pieced sashing strip, place pins vertically into the seams to match the sashing and block seams (Figure 5). Piece the sashing strips to the bottom of the first row. Fold back the sashing to verify the joint (Figure 6).

Press open the front seam allowance. Add the top of Row 2 to the sashing at the bottom of Row 1, carefully aligning the blocks and sashing strips (Figure 7). Pin carefully if using a pieced sashing strip. Continue piecing the rows into one large unit.

You can also use reversible piecing to attach borders to the edges of your quilts or to attach cornerstones to the borders.

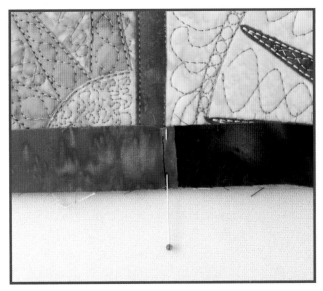

Piecing Rows Together, Figure 5

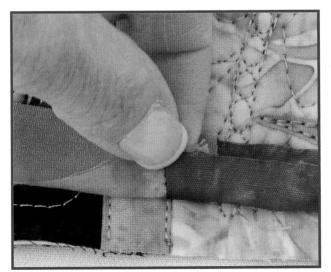

Piecing Rows Together, Figure 6

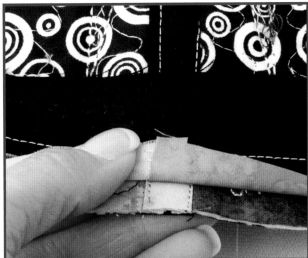

Piecing Rows Together, Figure 7

Easy Binding

The key to success for this fusible binding technique is cutting the strips after the paper-backed fusible web has been applied. This gives a clean, crisp finish to the edges. Start with fabric that is two times wider than the width of the finished binding, plus ⅛". The binding on this sample is ½". Cut the strips long enough to go around the perimeter of the quilt, plus 4".

To begin, press the fusible web to the fabric in the required length. It's fine to butt the edges of the web together (Figure 1).

Cut the fused strips to the appropriate width (here, 1⅛"), trimming on both sides of the fabric strip. You should slice off fusible web on both sides so the fusible web extends all the way to each edge of the strip (Figure 2).

Fold and press the strips in half lengthwise, matching the raw edges (Figure 3).

Lay the quilt, right side up, on a large pressing surface. Remove the protective paper from one binding strip. Slide the folded strip under the quilt edge, encasing the edge in the fold. Press the binding to the quilt top from the front (Figure 4). Flip the quilt over and press the back edge. Continue applying the binding to the quilt, overlapping one of the binding strips with the next. Miter the corners as you travel around the quilt (Figure 5).

NOTES FROM NANCY

If you'd like to add more stability to the binding, simply stitch along the inside folded edge.

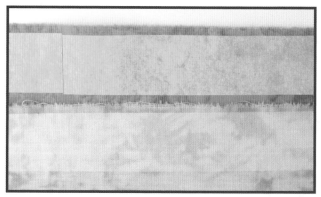

Easy Binding, Figure 1

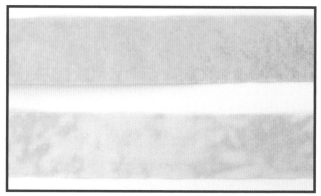

Easy Binding, Figure 2

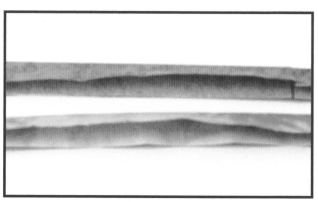

Easy Binding, Figure 3

Easy Binding, Figure 4

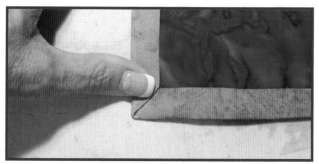

Easy Binding, Figure 5

Labels

You'll find designs for five different labels on the enclosed disk to use as you'd like to identify your creations. For my labels, I opened each label in lettering software in order to add the title of the quilt as well as my name, hometown and year. You could do the same, or stitch the blank label and write in the information. If you will be writing in the information, test your marker on a scrap of fabric before making the actual label.

To make a label, gather a 6" square of plain fabric that contrasts with the back of the quilt, paper-backed fusible web, fusible poly mesh stabilizer and a stencil cutter or wood-burning tool. I prefer to use a fusible poly mesh stabilizer when creating labels because it is very strong and will support the heavy satin-stitched edge. The heat-activated adhesive permanently secures the stabilizer to the label after the embroidery process, so I don't have to worry about the label (or a portion of it) becoming detached from the back of the quilt.

First, select the label design. Hoop the poly mesh stabilizer with the adhesive side up. Stitch color 1, the placement guide. Place a piece of fabric over the outline and stitch color 2, the tackdown. Carefully remove the hoop from the machine and trim the excess fabric.

Reattach the hoop to the machine and complete the design. Take the hooped stabilizer and label out of the hoop. Trim the stabilizer close to the satin stitch edge. Run a stencil cutter along the edge of the label to dissolve any remaining poly mesh stabilizer (Figure 1).

Press the label from the back, permanently fusing the two layers together. Place the label on a Teflon pressing sheet. Place a piece of paper-backed fusible web over the label and press. Trim the excess web. Peel off the protective paper. Place the label on the wrong side of the quilt and fuse (Figure 2).

Labels, Figure 1

Labels, Figure 2

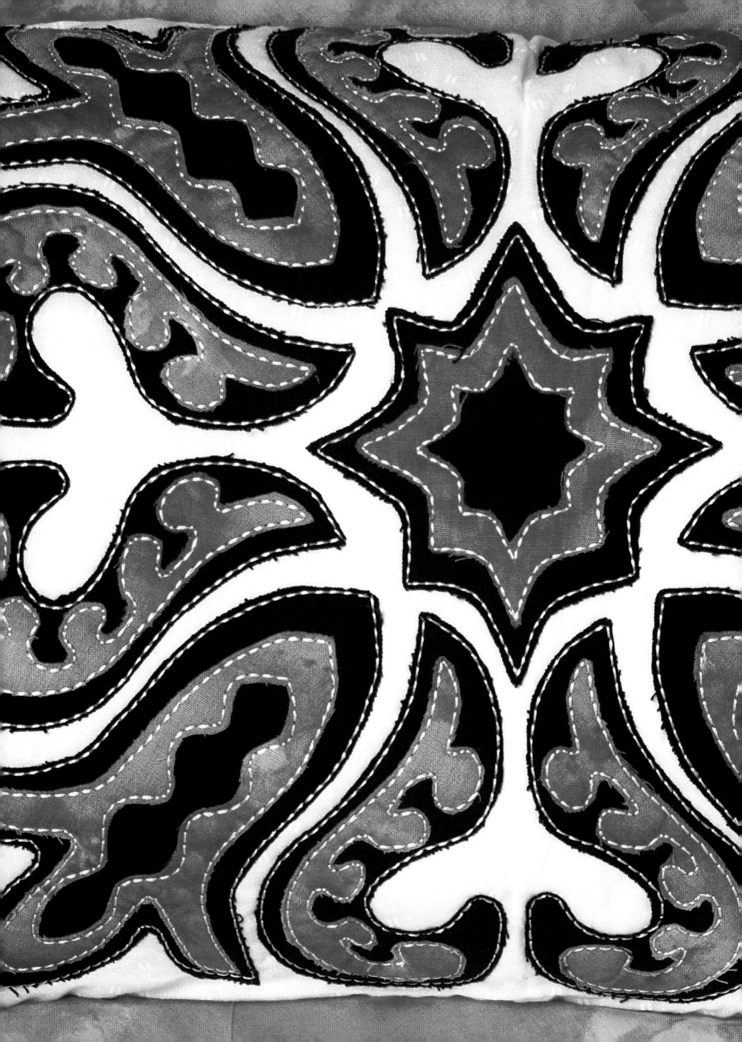

CHAPTER 5

Start Small

I think there's nothing better than the feeling of learning a new technique and finishing a project. So set yourself up for success and start small to familiarize yourself with these revolutionary techniques. I've included four small projects to help you get your feet wet.

The easiest project of all, the *Raggedy Edge Coasters* on page 44, will give you a taste of the technique. You'll become familiar with hooping a quilt sandwich, stitching the colors in the proper sequence, adding the appliqué fabric and finally trimming. This is a very rewarding project because one coaster stitches up in just 8 minutes—how's that for quick success?

The *No-Sew Pin Cushion* on page 48 includes raw edge appliqué in the form of several hearts nested inside of each other—a great way to incorporate multiple fabrics. The pin cushion is "no-sew" because it's finished entirely in the hoop. Once complete, you'll pop it out of the hoop and be done!

You'll step it up a notch when you tackle the *Pieced Pin Cushion* on page 52. This time, you'll stitch a front and back and sew them together with a strip of fabric. Of course, all of those seams are the perfect landing spot for luscious trims. And don't forget about the pins! I embellish my own with beads, and I tell you how on page 54. I love these pins, and they make a great addition to any pin cushion that you're gifting to someone dear.

If you're looking for impact, then the *Plume Pillow* on page 56 is for you. Wow—talk about pillow punch! I love this large block—it looks like you had a fancy-schmancy embroidery machine with a humongous hoop, but it's really made with multiple hoopings and some ingenious linking techniques that pull it all together. It's a powerful decorative element for any room.

Raggedy Edge Coasters

FINISHED SIZE: 4½" × 4½"

This project uses the following file: CoasterF1

These lovely coasters make a wonderful hostess gift. You can stitch up a set of four in under 35 minutes! Consider using a multitude of color combinations. I chose hot, tropical colors perfect for a pool party, but you can design yours to coordinate with any decorating scheme. The organic style of the appliqué design blends with many different looks—everything from highly contrasting black-and-white to soothing earth tones.

GATHER THESE ITEMS (FOR 4 COASTERS)

Base fabric: four 9" × 12" pieces of loose-weave fabric, such as linen

Appliqué fabric: four 3" squares

Batting: two 9" × 12" pieces

4" × 4" hoop

HOOP THE MATERIALS

Sandwich the batting between the two pieces of loose-weave fabric. Place the quilt sandwich in the hoop with one short edge of the quilt sandwich just beyond the top of the hoop. Hoop the fabric so the crosswise grain is parallel with the edge of the hoop. Hooping the fabric on the grain will produce an even frayed edge on the coasters.

STITCH THE COASTERS

Embroider color 1, the square outline. Embroider colors 2 and 3, changing thread colors if desired (Figure 1). Place the appliqué fabric over the coaster design after completing color 3 (Figure 2). Stitch color 4, the appliqué tackdown, and color 5, the decorative stitching (Figure 3).

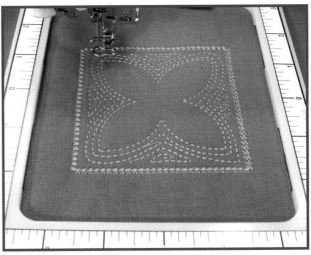

Stitch the Coasters, Figure 1

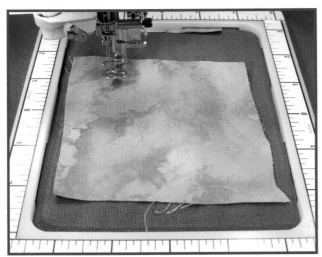

Stitch the Coasters, Figure 2

Stitch the Coasters, Figure 3

Stitch the Coasters, Figure 4

Lift the hoop's top frame and slide the quilt sandwich up to expose a clean area of fabric. Use the machine's trace feature to position the needle at the top of the design. Measure the distance from the needle position to the lower edge of the previously stitched coaster. Make sure there is at least 1½" between the designs (Figure 4). If not, move the fabric in the hoop.

Repeat the process to make four coasters.

TRIM AND FRAY THE COASTERS

Trim the appliqué fabric on each design. Trim each coaster leaving a ½" seam allowance on all sides (Figure 1).

Starting at one side, fold down the front and back fabric of the coaster to expose the batting. Trim the batting close to the stitching line, being careful not to nip the fabric (Figure 2). Repeat for all four sides of each coaster.

To make the frayed edge, pull a thread to release it from the weave. Keep pulling threads on all four sides to create the frayed edge (Figure 3).

Trim and Fray the Coasters, Figure 1

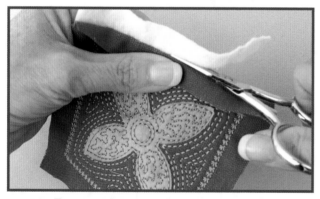

Trim and Fray the Coasters, Figure 2

NOTES FROM NANCY

When you need a quick hostess or birthday gift, keep the *Raggedy Edge Coasters* in mind. They're speedy to create, plus make an impressive gift!

Trim and Fray the Coasters, Figure 3

No-Sew Pin Cushion

FINISHED SIZE: 3½" × 3½"

This project uses the following file: Heart Cushion AppF3

No sewing is required for this pin cushion because it's all finished in the hoop. Dimension is added after all embroidery is complete—just slit the back, stuff and fuse the opening shut. Now that's a fast and easy no-sew pin cushion!

✹ Shopping Tip ✹

Select a tear-away stabilizer that rips away cleanly. The stabilizer should feel crisp in your hand, not soft.

GATHER THESE ITEMS

Appliqué fabrics: five 5" squares of cotton fabric

Backing fabric: 5" square of cotton fabric

5" × 7" hoop (you can use a 4" × 4" hoop, but a larger hoop makes it easier to trim the appliqué in the hoop)

Lightweight tear-away stabilizer

Polyester fiberfill

Temporary spray adhesive

STITCH THE PIN CUSHION

Hoop the lightweight tear-away stabilizer. Place a 5" square of appliqué fabric in the center of the hoop. Stitch color 1 (Figure 1).

Lay a second piece of appliqué fabric over the outline. Stitch colors 2 and 3 (Figure 2).

Lay a third piece of appliqué fabric over the outline and stitch color 4 (Figure 3).

Stitch the Pin Cushion, Figure 1

Creating Eileen's pincushion is a little like being part of a magic show! The embroidery is fascinating to watch as the layers are added and then stitched. With the backing of the pincushion cleverly added to the underside of the hoop, you'll soon realize that you've learned an embroidery slight of hand!

NOTES FROM NANCY

Stitch the Pin Cushion, Figure 2

Stitch the Pin Cushion, Figure 3

Lay a fourth piece of appliqué fabric over the outline and stitch color 5 (Figure 4). Stitch color 6 as well. Lay the fifth and final piece of appliqué fabric over the outline. Take the time to center an interesting motif, if desired. Stitch color 7 (Figure 5).

Carefully remove the hoop from the machine. Trim the excess fabric from the appliqués so they are not extending beyond the large heart stitched by color 1 (Figure 6).

Spray the wrong side of the 5" square of backing fabric with temporary adhesive. Smooth the tacky surface to the back of the hoop, covering the large heart outline (Figure 7).

Reattach the hoop to the machine and stitch the next color, the tackdown. Remove the hoop from the machine. Trim the large heart on the front and back of the hoop (Figure 8).

Reattach the hoop and stitch the final color, the satin stitch outline (Figure 9). Remove the hoop from the machine and unhoop the stabilizer. Tear the pin cushion from the tear-away stabilizer.

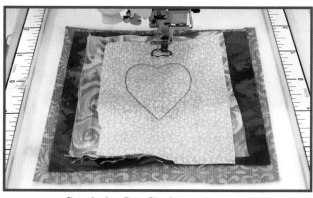

Stitch the Pin Cushion, Figure 4

Stitch the Pin Cushion, Figure 5

Stitch the Pin Cushion, Figure 6

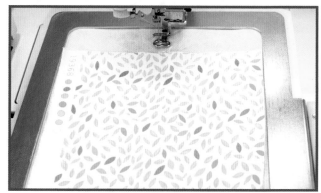

Stitch the Pin Cushion, Figure 7

Stitch the Pin Cushion, Figure 8

Stitch the Pin Cushion, Figure 9

FINISH THE PIN CUSHION

Use a seam ripper to poke a hole in the back layer of the pin cushion. Slide the blades of a small pair of scissors into the opening and cut a slit in the form of an X (Figure 1).

Stuff the pin cushion with polyester fiberfill (Figure 2) . Fuse a scrap of fabric over the opening (Figure 3).

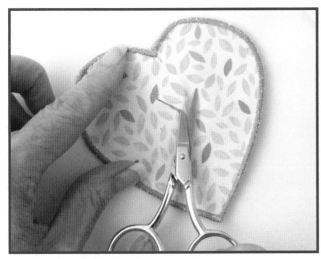

Finish the Pin Cushion, Figure 1

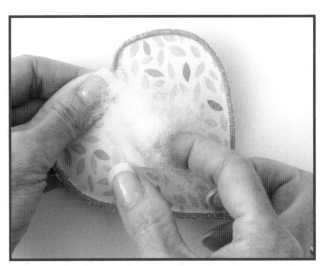

Finish the Pin Cushion, Figure 2

Finish the Pin Cushion, Figure 3

Pieced Pin Cushion

FINISHED SIZE: 3¾" × 3¾"

This project uses the following files: Heart Pin CushionF1, Heart Pin Cushion BackF1, HeartPatchF1

Oh, the charm of pin cushions! I adore this small canvas—so fun to decorate, so easy to create, so lovely to hold in the palm of your hand. I love mixing colorful fabrics and textured trims no matter what I'm working on, but the best part about pin cushions is that you only need a small amount of supplies. But wow—do those supplies go a long way! Proceed with caution: this project can be addictive!

HOOP THE MATERIALS

Make a quilt cracker with batting and base fabric. Because the piece of batting is smaller than the fabric, align the top edge of the batting with the top edge of the fabric. Hoop the quilt cracker, aligning the cracker's top edge with the top edge of the hoop.

START STITCHING

Begin stitching file Heart Pin CushionF1. Stitch color 1, the pin cushion outline. After stitching color 1, place a piece of appliqué fabric over the outline, then stitch color 2, the tackdown, and color 3, the inner stipple (Figure 1).

After color 3 is complete, place a contrasting piece of appliqué fabric over the outline. Stitch color 4, the tackdown (Figure 2). After color 4 is complete, place another piece of appliqué fabric over the outline. Stitch color 5, the tackdown, and color 6, the inner stipple.

After color 6 is complete, place the last piece of appliqué fabric over the heart. Because this entire piece of appliqué fabric will be seen, take the time to center an interesting motif. Stitch color 7, the tackdown (Figure 3).

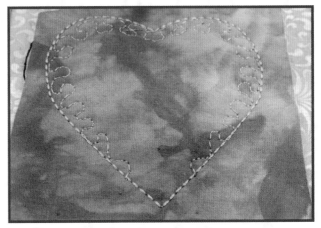

Start Stitching, Figure 1

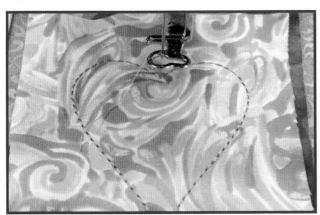

Start Stitching, Figure 2

Start Stitching, Figure 3

Lift the hoop frame and center a clean area of the fabric in the hoop for the heart back, keeping the batting free and leaving at least 1" between the heart front design and the heart back. Because the heart back design is only an outline, it's not necessary to use stabilizer or batting. Stitch the file Heart Pin Cushion BackF1 on this fabric (Figure 4). Remove it from the hoop.

Hoop the panel and patch fabric. No stabilizer is necessary. Stitch the file HeartPatchF1. Remove the fabric from the hoop. Cut a 14" × 2" strip from the panel and patch fabric for the side panel. Set this strip aside. Iron paper-backed fusible web to the wrong side of the heart patch. Remove the protective paper and trim the heart, leaving an ⅛" seam allowance (Figure 5).

Trim the excess batting from the back of the heart front (Figure 6). Trim the appliqués on the heart front, cutting close to the stitching line (Figure 7).

Start Stitching, Figure 4

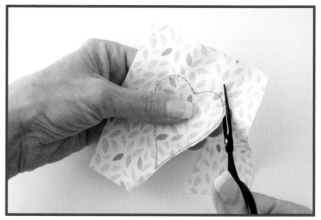

Start Stitching, Figure 5

Start Stitching, Figure 6

Start Stitching, Figure 7

❀ Gift Giving ❀

Giving a pin cushion as a gift? Top it off with show-stopping pins! I love making my own pins—you can see some of mine in action on page 76. To make your own, start with a fine, sharp 1⅞" crystal glass head pin. Place a drop of craft glue or permanent glue on the glass head. Slide a pretty bead onto the pin and down to the head. Add another drop of glue to the bottom of the bead. Slide a second bead on. Add a third bead if you wish and end with a dollop of glue.

Hold the pin upside down for a moment until the glue sets. Put a 5" square of cork board on top of a coffee mug and insert the pins on the underside of the cork. Gravity will do its work, and the glue will set permanently. Let the pins set for an hour or two to dry completely.

Trim the heart back. Fold the heart in half and snip into the center leaving a ¼" seam allowance. Trim the inside heart (Figure 8). You will use this opening to turn and stuff the pin cushion.

ASSEMBLE THE PIN CUSHION

Sew the short ends of the side panel strip, right sides together, with ¼" seam allowance to form a tube. Pin the side panel strip RST to the heart back, placing the side panel seam at the center top of the heart. Sew with ¼" seam allowance (Figure 1).

Clip the seam allowance. Repeat to add the heart front. Turn the pin cushion right side out through the heart-shaped opening and stuff the pin cushion with fiberfill (Figure 2). Place the heart patch over the opening and fuse in place.

EMBELLISH THE PIN CUSHION

Use a hot glue gun to add the ball trim to the center of the side panel. Finish the top edge with two rows of mini rickrack (Figure 1). Hot glue or hand-sew in place.

Start Stitching, Figure 8

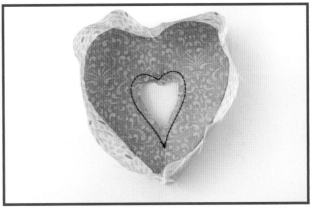

Assemble the Pin Cushion, Figure 1

Assemble the Pin Cushion, Figure 2

Embellish the Pin Cushion, Figure 1

Shorten the stitch length to 12–15 stitches when sewing the side panel strip to the front and back of the pin cushion. It will be easier to maneuver the curves, plus it gives the seam extra strength.

NOTES FROM NANCY

Plume Pillow

FINISHED SIZE: 11½" × 21½"

This project uses the following files: PlumeCtrF1, Plume2F1

The bold shapes of the *Plume Pillow*'s appliqués make quite a statement in any décor. Choose colors that blend—or contrast—with your room. Adding paper-backed fusible web to the appliqué fabrics ensures the pillow will stand up to the normal wear and tear of everyday use. Make one today and introduce a splash of color into your décor!

PREPARE MATERIALS

Fuse paper-backed fusible web to the wrong side of the coral and black fabrics. Cut two 15" × 25" pieces from the base and backing fabric, one 15" × 25" piece of batting and one 11" × 23" piece of base and backing fabric (for the pillow back). Press the horizontal and vertical centers of the 15" × 25" pieces of fabric. Make sure the creases are highly visible. If they are not, I recommend marking them with removable marker. Layer the pressed fabrics with batting.

STITCH THE PILLOW TOP

Hoop the upper right quadrant of the quilt sandwich. Make sure the crease lines are at the outer edge of the sewing field. Load file Plume2F1. Using the trace feature on the machine, position the needle at the lower left point of the design area. Adjust as needed until the needle is positioned directly over the spot where the creases intersect. Move the design 10mm up from the horizontal crease and 10mm to the right of the vertical crease (Figure 1).

Embroider color 1, the alignment marks (Figure 2). Place one end of the 6" black strip over the design area. Stitch color 2 (Figure 3).

Base and backing fabric: 1 yd. white cotton fabric

Appliqué fabrics: one 6" × 30" strip each, black and coral

Binding: ¼ yd. contrasting or coordinating cotton fabric

Batting: one 15" × 25" piece

5" × 7" hoop

10" × 20" pillow form

Paper-backed fusible web

2¼ yd. of ¹²/₃₂" fusible piping

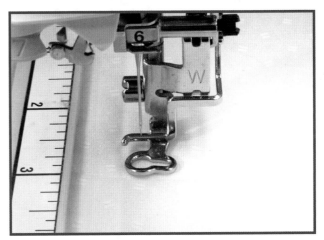

Stitch the Pillow Top, Figure 1

Stitch the Pillow Top, Figure 2

Stitch the Pillow Top, Figure 3

Stitch the Pillow Top, Figure 4

Place one end of the 6" coral strip over the design area and stitch color 3 (Figure 4). Remove the quilt sandwich from the hoop. Right now, the alignment marks are obstructed by the appliqué fabrics. Trim the excess appliqué fabrics on the sides where the next repeats will connect so you can view the alignment marks.

Hoop the next quadrant. Use the alignment marks as a guide when positioning the quilt sandwich in the hoop. The alignment marks need to be 20mm away from and parallel to the alignment marks on the first design. Use the trace feature to travel from the lower left to the middle left and upper left points of the design. This verifies the quilt sandwich is square in the hoop. If any adjustments are needed, make them now. Stitch color 1, the alignment marks (Figure 5).

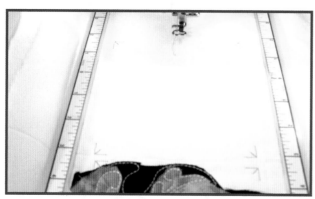

Stitch the Pillow Top, Figure 5

Repeat the embroidery process for all four quadrants (Figure 6). Continually check your progress, making sure the alignment marks are evenly spaced and square.

Continue in the same manner for the quilting designs on each side of the large block. The designs and spacing are the same as the large block, but without appliqué fabric (Figure 7).

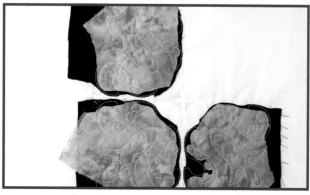

Stitch the Pillow Top, Figure 6

Trim the excess appliqué fabric around the outside of the stitching. Place the scissor blade close to the stitching and cleanly clip the fabric. Insert the tip of a seam ripper into just the top layer of appliqué in the center of each design (Figure 8).

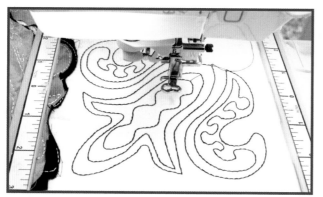

Stitch the Pillow Top, Figure 7

Stitch the Pillow Top, Figure 8

Once a small hole is made, slip the point of a scissors into the opening and slice down the center. Trim close to the stitching (Figure 9).

Place the pillow top on a flat surface and center a target ruler on the center opening. Make sure the vertical and horizontal lines on the ruler are evenly spaced between the appliqué designs. Insert a target sticker into the hole, aligning the sticker's crosshair with the ruler's crosshair (Figure 10). Verify the positioning by placing the PlumeCtrF1 template on the crosshair (Figure 11). Check the outer edges. Are they evenly spaced in the openings? Make any necessary adjustments.

Hoop the pillow front, centering the target sticker in the design area. Load file PlumeCtrF1. I recommend using the trace feature to verify the fabric is square in the hoop. Move the needle to the outer four points: top, left, bottom and right (Figure 12).

Stitch the Pillow Top, Figure 9

Stitch the Pillow Top, Figure 10

Stitch the Pillow Top, Figure 11

Stitch the Pillow Top, Figure 12

Stitch the Pillow Top, Figure 13

Place a piece of black appliqué fabric over the design area and stitch color 1. Place a piece of coral appliqué fabric over the design area and stitch color 2 (Figure 13). Trim the center design (Figure 14). After all trimming is completed, heat-bond the appliqué fabrics to the base following the fusible web manufacturer's directions for pressing. Centering the design area, trim the pillow top to 11" × 21".

ASSEMBLE THE PILLOW

Cut one 64" length of 2⅝"-wide bias strip from the binding fabric. (This includes a ½" seam allowance). Wrap the bias strip around the fusible piping. Press with a dry iron in the seam allowance only. Do not fuse the last 4" of the bias strip.

Starting with the fused end, align the raw edge of the cord with the raw edge of the pillow. Attach a zipper foot to your sewing machine. Start sewing 2" from the fused end and continue around the pillow front. Clip into the seam allowance of the cord ½" from the corner (Figure 1).

Pinch the cord to turn the corner. Leaving the needle in the fabric, lift the presser foot and pivot the fabric to turn the corner. Continue to stitch around the corner (Figure 2).

Stitch the Pillow Top, Figure 14

Assemble the Pillow, Figure 1

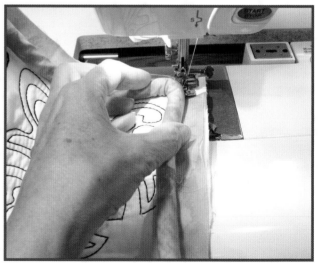

Assemble the Pillow, Figure 2

To finish the ends of the cord, stop stitching about 3" from your start point. Peel back the bias covering from the opposite end to expose the cord (Figure 3). Butt the ends of the cord together and snip the exposed end (Figure 4). Fold the short raw edge of the bias strip and finger press. Insert the other end of the cord into the bias strip, covering the end of the cord with the strip. Stitch.

Create an opening in the pillow back using the method of your choice. You can add a zipper, buttons or snaps to the opening, or you can create an envelope back if you like. Place the pillow back and front right sides together. Sew with the pillow front facing up. Stitch inside of the stitching line. Trim the corners. Turn right side out and insert the pillow form.

Assemble the Pillow, Figure 3

Assemble the Pillow, Figure 4

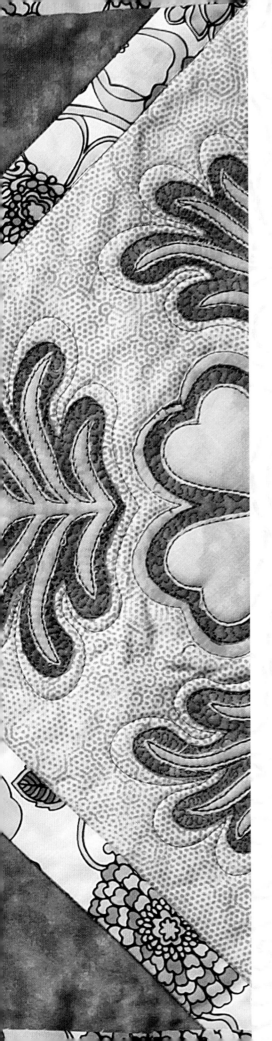

CHAPTER 6

Step It Up

The projects in this chapter are precious, and they are an interesting combination of finished items and techniques. Trapunto is what elevates the table runner on page 64. It's a fun technique to try and can be incorporated into many other projects. You'll learn how to hide the batting, add appliqué, lay out a large block and accent a decorative fabric. Remember to let your appliqué fabrics be the stars—use the accent fabric sparingly because a little goes a long way.

The *Scallop Tote* on page 72 features the continuous appliqué technique, but this time the appliqué is the finished edge of the tote. Imagine how cool it would look as a finished edge on a quilt! Remember that all of the techniques and embroidery designs can be mixed, giving you complete freedom to come up with your projects. Once you finish the *Scallop Tote*, you'll be tempted to apply those techniques to other projects.

My Favorite Bag on page 78 is, well, my favorite bag! I love the shape, the grommets, the swirl quilting designs and the fabrics. The touch of coral and aqua breathe such life into the muted base fabrics. I had a blast designing the strap and dreaming up a solution for how to hold the straps onto the bag. Wooden dowels and a little decoupage to the rescue! It was like arts and crafts back in grade school.

The *Sewing Notions Caddy* on page 86 looks elegant in any sewing room. In my sewing room, it's a splash of sunny, summer color all year long. I love the pop of the paisley fabric and the gentle curve of the scallop trim. It started as a simple coffee can but has now been promoted to a wonderful new life as the holder of my scissors, rulers, rotary cutters and the like. If yours wants to topple over from the weight of some of your larger scissors, consider putting rice in the bottom of the caddy. The rice won't hurt anything, and the added weight will balance the caddy.

When you're ready to step up from the basics and venture out into truly revolutionary results, you're ready to dive into this chapter!

Trapunto Table Runner

FINISHED SIZE: 17¾" × 55"

This project uses the following files: CornerF1, Fleur de lisF1, Fleur De Lis CenterF1

The color scheme of this table runner started with the floral fabric in the sashing and binding—what a unique fabric! The fresh aqua and lime fabrics breathe fresh air into the humdrum tan and brown earthtones. Try playing with bursts of color like this in your décor to freshen up your space.

PREPARE MATERIALS

Open the designs for this project in embroidery editing software and print templates of each design. Draw an arrow on each template to designate the top of the design (Figure 1). Cut out the templates.

MAKE THE ON-POINT BLOCKS

Make three identical 18"-square quilt sandwiches. Press each layer. Fuse the three layers together with temporary spray adhesive if desired, or just stack the three layers together. Draw a 12" square in the center of each quilt sandwich. Press two diagonal lines from corner to corner (Figure 1). Place the Fleur De Lis CenterF1 template in the center of the block (Figure 2).

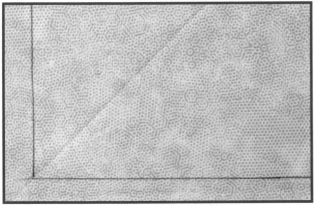

Prepare Materials, Figure 1

✹ Hands-On Embroidery ✹

For this project, it's wise to stay with the machine during the stitching process so you can keep an eye on the lofty appliqué. To avoid puckers in the appliqué fabric, use the eraser end of a pencil to hold the appliqué fabric taut during stitching.

If you use high-loft poly batting for the trapunto areas, place a piece of water-soluble stabilizer over the batting. This will stop the embroidery foot from getting tangled in the loose weave of the batting.

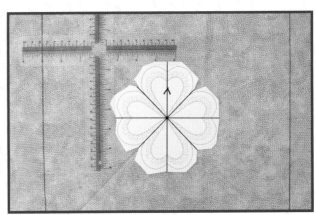

Make the On-Point Blocks, Figure 1   *Make the On-Point Blocks, Figure 2*

To mark the position of the four corner designs, use a target ruler to add the corner templates. Place the ruler so the 3" mark hits the edge of the 12" block, both vertically and horizontally. Slide the Fleur de LisF1 template over the target ruler (Figure 3). Make sure the template's crosshair is centered on the target ruler. Look at the arrow you drew on the template to make sure the design will stitch in the proper direction.

Remove the template and place a target sticker in the hole of the target ruler. Make sure the arrow points toward the top of the intended direction of the design. Repeat for the remaining three corners (Figures 4–5). When you are finished, you will have five target stickers on the block (Figure 6).

Hoop the block center. Position the needle over the center target sticker crosshair. Place a 6" square of aqua fabric in the center of the hoop. Begin stitching Fleur De Lis CenterF1. Stitch color 1, the tackdown of the large appliqué (Figure 7).

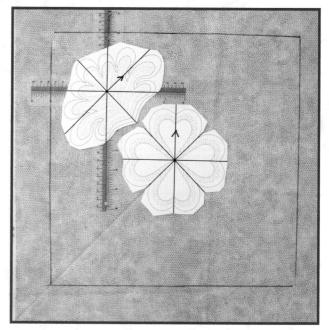

Make the On-Point Blocks, Figure 3

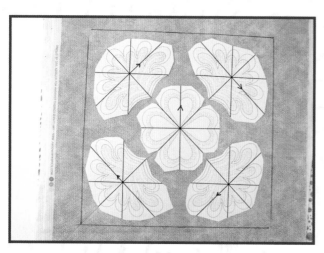

Make the On-Point Blocks, Figure 4

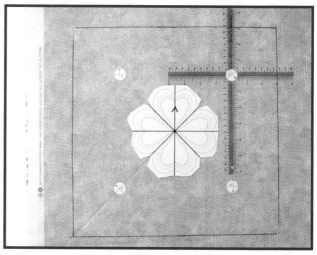

Make the On-Point Blocks, Figure 5

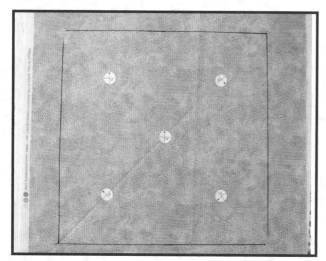

Make the On-Point Blocks, Figure 6

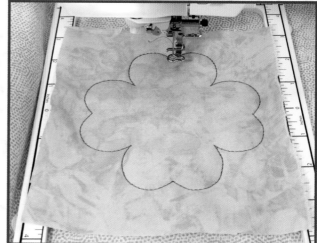

Make the On-Point Blocks, Figure 7

After completing color 1, place a 5" square of batting over the outline (Figure 8). Stitch color 2, the tackdown of the trapunto batting. Remove the hoop from the machine after stitching color 2. Trim the batting close to the stitched outline (Figure 9).

Place a 6" square of brown appliqué fabric over the large outline and reattach the hoop to the machine. Stitch color 3, the tackdown of the brown appliqué. Stitch color 4, the stipple inside the large appliqué (Figure 10).

After completing color 4, place a 6" square of lime appliqué fabric over the center design. Stitch color 5, the tackdown of the small appliqué (Figure 11).

Once the center motif is finished, you'll begin working on the Fleur de LisF1 motifs. Hoop the quilt block on the diagonal so the target sticker crosshair is square in the hoop (Figure 12).

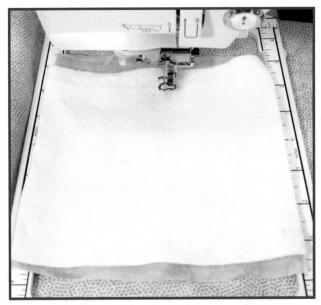

Make the On-Point Blocks, Figure 8

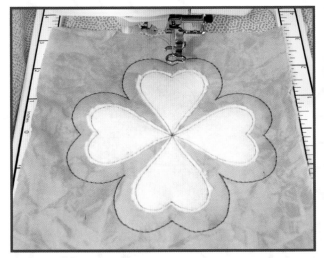

Make the On-Point Blocks, Figure 9

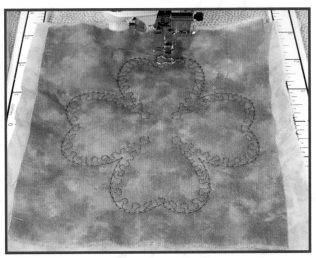

Make the On-Point Blocks, Figure 10

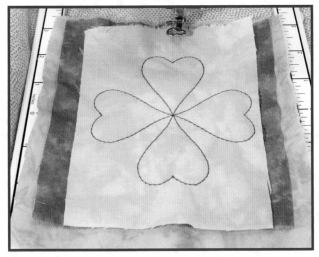

Make the On-Point Blocks, Figure 11

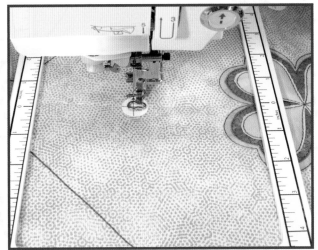

Make the On-Point Blocks, Figure 12

67

Select the Fleur de LisF1 design on your embroidery machine. Position the needle over the target sticker. This is a fairly large design (107mm × 160mm), so the degree of rotation may be limited. Notice the orientation of the design. To verify the position, place the template on the target sticker. For added insurance, place a target ruler over the template to make sure the fabric is square in the hoop (Figure 13).

If the fabric is not properly aligned, use an Angle Finder to find the degree of required rotation. After rotating the design in the center of the hoop, move the hoop by using the jog keys on the machine. Position the needle over the target sticker. Stitch the first color, the outline (Figure 14).

After completing color 1, place a 4½" × 6½" piece of brown appliqué fabric over the outline. Stitch color 2, the tackdown of the appliqué. Stitch color 3, the stipple (Figure 15). Place a 4½" × 6½" piece of aqua appliqué fabric over the stipple area. Stitch color 4, the tackdown of the interior appliqué (Figure 16).

Repeat this process for each corner design. Trim the appliqué fabrics once the block is removed from the hoop.

Make a total of three blocks. Trim the blocks to 13" square by adding a ½" seam allowance around the 12" square drawn on the base fabric.

NOTES FROM NANCY

An old Russian proverb states, "Measure twice; cut once." When embroidering you could slightly change these wise words to read, "Measure twice; embroider once!" Follow Eileen's guideline to verify the position of the template by measuring—measuring twice!

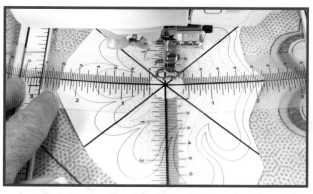

Make the On-Point Blocks, Figure 13

Make the On-Point Blocks, Figure 14

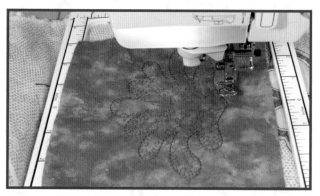

Make the On-Point Blocks, Figure 15

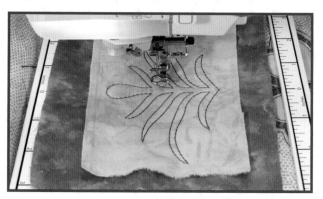

Make the On-Point Blocks, Figure 16

CREATE THE TRIANGLES

All four triangle sections for this quilt are stitched on one quilt sandwich. Stitch all embroidery before cutting the block into triangles.

Cut the backing, batting and base fabric to 22" × 22". Layer the materials to form a quilt sandwich. Draw an 18" square in the center of the base fabric. Position the edge of the ruler on the diagonal of the block running from corner to corner. Chalk this line. Flip the ruler to the opposite corners and chalk another diagonal 45-degree line. The block should now have a large X in the center. Add marks for ½" seam allowances to each side of the X.

For each triangle, place the 4" marks of the arms of a target ruler on the chalk lines dividing the square in four (not the seam allowance lines). Insert a target sticker into the hole.

Hoop the block, centering one target sticker in the sewing field. Use an Angle Finder to determine the degree of rotation required, if any. Rotate the design if necessary. Position the needle over the crosshair by using the jog keys. Remove the target sticker. Stitch the CornerF1 design starting with color 1, the outline (Figure 1).

Place batting over the stitched outline. Stitch color 2, the tackdown of the batting. Remove the hoop from the machine and carefully trim the excess batting (Figure 2).

Place a 6" square of lime appliqué fabric over the outline and stitch color 3, the tackdown of the large heart. Stitch color 4, the stipple (Figure 3). Once color 4 is complete, place a 6" square of aqua appliqué fabric over the outline and stitch color 5, the small heart tackdown (Figure 4).

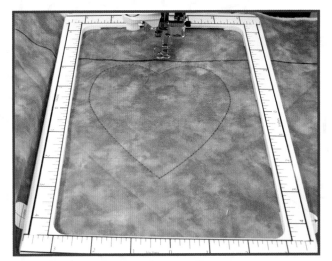

Create the Triangles, Figure 1

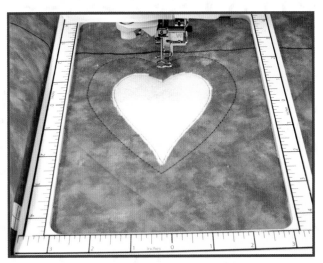

Create the Triangles, Figure 2

Create the Triangles, Figure 3

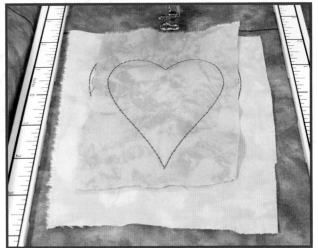

Create the Triangles, Figure 4

69

Assembling the Runner, Figure 1

Assembling the Runner, Figure 2

Assembling the Runner, Figure 3

Repeat for all four designs, rehooping the quilt sandwich as necessary. Trim all excess fabrics once the block is removed from the hoop.

Cut away the excess fabric outside of the marked 18" square. Place a quilter's ruler on the marked X to cut the square into four equal triangles. Before actually slicing the block, make sure the seam allowances are ½".

ASSEMBLING THE RUNNER

Cut from the sashing fabric: eight 12½" × 2" front sashing strips, four 12½" × 2" back sashing strips, two 25 " × 2" back sashing strips. Cut from the aqua fabric: two 2" × 2"cornerstones.

Lay out the triangle sections and on-point blocks on a design wall using the photo on page 71 as a placement guide. Take the on-point block from one end and the adjoining triangle section to your sewing machine. Use reversible piecing (see pages 36–39) to piece together a triangle section and an on-point block with ½" seam allowances. Sewing these pieces in the proper order will help stabilize the bias edge of the pieces. Begin by piecing sashing strips cut to exactly 13" long (front and back) to the diagonal edge of the triangle section, easing the bias edges to fit as needed. Attach an on-point block to the opposite edge of the sashing (Figure 1). Return this pieced section to the design wall.

Select the next triangle section, the center on-point block, and the next triangle section from the design wall. Piece these three sections together using reversible piecing, again adding the sashing strips to the triangles and then the square block (Figure 2). Piece together the last triangle and on-point block in the same manner (Figure 3).

Make two pieced front sashing strips to go between the rows (see page 38). These sashing strips are composed of two front sashing strips separated by a cornerstone. Assemble the rows using reversible piecing to form the full runner. Bind the quilt using a traditional method or the super-fast, fusible binding method (see page 40).

71

Scallop Tote

FINISHED SIZE: 12¾" × 12¾" × 3½" (EXCLUDING HANDLES)

This project uses the following files: Grid oneLineF1, ContScallopCircF1

A charming scalloped edge adds personality to this colorful tote bag. Perfect to sling over your shoulder on shopping day, it's ample enough to carry a loaf of bread and bunches of vegetables and fruits. Or maybe you'd prefer to transport knitting needles and balls of yarn. Whatever you decide to put in it, you'll be proud to carry this bag.

MAKE THE GRID STRIP

Cut an 11" × WOF piece of the bottom panel fabric, batting and backing. Assemble these three pieces to make a quilt sandwich. Place a 45" length of painter's tape along the long side of the quilt sandwich.

The Grid oneLineF1 design will be stitched horizontally, from left to right, on this quilt sandwich. Hoop the left side of the quilt sandwich using the painter's tape at the top edge as a guide. Keep ¼" of the tape inside of the hoop. This will make a highly visible alignment guide on any type of fabric.

Select and stitch the Grid oneLineF1 design. Skip color 1 (a vertical alignment line unnecessary for this first grid) and stitch colors 2 and 3 (Figure 1). Color 3 is a straight vertical line on the right side of the grid. This line is used for alignment. Lift the top frame of the hoop or rehoop the fabric. Slide the next embroidery field into position, keeping the stitched alignment line within the left portion of the sewing field and parallel to the hoop.

On the machine's editing screen, advance to the first stitch. The needle should be positioned directly over the top of the alignment line (Figure 2). Advance 10–20 stitches, keeping an eye on the center of the embroidery foot. It should travel directly over the stitched line. If not, adjust the fabric so the line is aligned with the machine foot. Advance to the bottom of the line, checking the alignment as the foot travels down the line (Figure 3).

GATHER THESE ITEMS

Bottom panel fabric: ⅔ yd.

Top panel and sashing fabric: ½ yd.

Appliqué and lining fabric: ⅓ yd.

Backing: ½ yd.

Batting: 32" × 45"

5" × 7" hoop

Painter's tape

Two 17" leather purse handles

Paper-backed fusible web

16" piece of ribbon

Make the Grid Strip, Figure 1

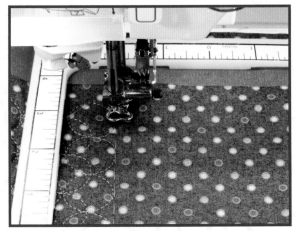

Make the Grid Strip, Figure 2

Make the Grid Strip, Figure 3

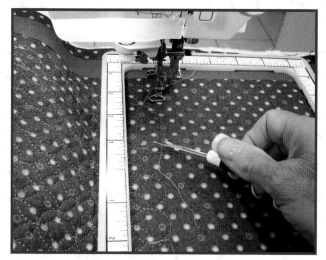

Make the Grid Strip, Figure 4

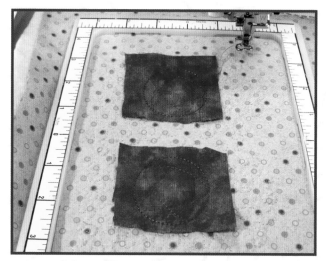

Stitch the Scallop Strip, Figure 1

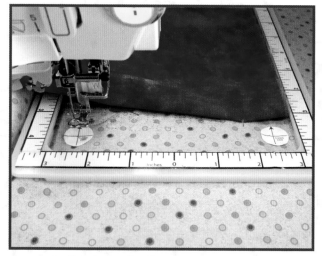

Stitch the Scallop Strip, Figure 2

Advance to color 2 (stitch 29); the needle will be positioned over the previously stitched circles. Use a seam ripper to remove the straight line of stitches (Figure 4).

Stitch Grid oneLineF1 again. If you choose, you can stitch color 1 to verify that the new design will be perfectly aligned, but I didn't find that was necessary. Traveling through the stitches as described above gave me enough confidence to continue stitching.

Fill the quilt sandwich with seven repeats of Grid oneLineF1. Make and hoop an 11" × 25" quilt sandwich of bottom panel fabric, batting and backing, and stitch three repeats of Grid oneLineF1 for the bag bottom.

Trim the quilted strip ½" from both long edges of the quilting. Trim the length to 33½". The trimmed strip measures 33½" × 8". Cut the smaller quilted strip to 4½" × 13¾" for the bag bottom.

STITCH THE SCALLOP STRIP

Cut a 3" × 30" strip of appliqué fabric. Fuse paper-backed fusible web to the wrong side of the appliqué fabric. Cut the fusible-backed appliqué fabric into ten 3" squares.

Make a 9" × WOF quilt cracker of top panel fabric and batting. The ContScallopCircF1 design will be stitched horizontally from left to right. Hoop the left side of the strip. Stitch color 1 of the ContScallopCircF1 design, the stipple stitches. Place a square of fusible-backed appliqué fabric over each hole in the stipple pattern and stitch colors 2 and 3, the tackdown and dot embellishment (Figure 1). Trim the lower edges of the dot appliqués so they don't extend beyond the stipple stitches.

Lay the top edge of a 7" × WOF strip of lining fabric over the design, right side down. A ½" of fabric should extend beyond the scallop-shaped side. Stitch color 4, the scallop outline.

Lift the lining fabric back over the design. Use the trace feature to position the needle over the lower left corner of the design. Place a target sticker under the needle. Position the needle over the lower right corner of the design and place a target sticker under the needle (Figure 2).

Carefully lift the top frame of the hoop and slide the fabric over to the next unstitched section or rehoop the fabric. Don't dislodge the target stickers while moving the fabric. Use the trace feature to position the needle at what is now the top left corner of the design.

Place the needle directly over the target sticker. Use the flywheel to manually drop the needle (Figure 3). The needle should pierce the target sticker in the center of the crosshair. If it doesn't, use one of the following methods to position the needle correctly: use the jog keys to move the hoop, reposition the fabric by gently tugging on the fabric, or lift the hoop's top frame and move the fabric or rehoop the fabric. Move the needle to the top right corner and check its placement as you did for the left side.

Keep the strip of lining fabric out of the design area and stitch the first three colors of ContScallopCircF1. Smooth the lining fabric into place, keeping the right edge flat after completing color 3. It's okay if the fabric does not lie flat in the hoop on the left side (Figure 4). Once the hoop is removed, the scallop will be flat.

Stitch color 4, the scallop. Stitch tContScallopCircF1 five times on the strip. Remove the strip from the hoop.

Trim the scalloped edge approximately ⅛" from the stitching (Figure 5). Clip around the scallops and into the peak of each scallop, being careful not to clip the stitches.

Place the ½" line of a quilter's ruler on the edge of the stitching on the remaining long side and slice away the excess fabric and batting. Cut the width of the strip to 33½". The trimmed strip measures 33½" × 5½" at the widest part of the scallops.

Turn the border right side out using a point turner. Carefully insert the point turner into each curved scallop and smooth the seam. Allow an even amount of lining fabric to peek out from the back. Press the scallop border edge and, at the same time, heat-bond the appliqués following the fusible web manufacturer's directions.

Stitch the Scallop Strip, Figure 3

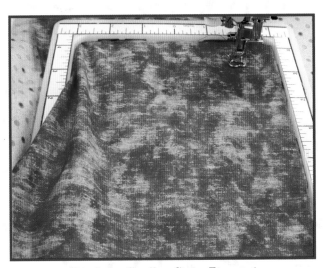
Stitch the Scallop Strip, Figure 4

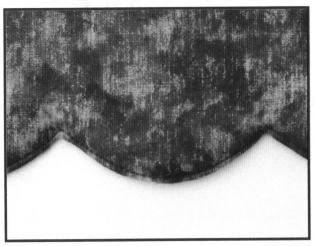
Stitch the Scallop Strip, Figure 5

NOTES FROM **NANCY**

If your fabric has a tendency to ravel, consider stitching the scallop embroidery stitch twice. The extra stitching will prevent the fabric from unraveling after the trimming step.

ASSEMBLE THE TOTE

Cut 2" × 34" front and back sashing strips. I opted to use the same fabric as the scallop border so the sashing would not introduce another design element. You can go this route if you choose, or use a contrasting fabric to add to your design. Sew the scallop panel to the bottom panel with the reversible piecing technique (see pages 36–39) (Figure 1).

One of the challenges of a scalloped border is the join of one short end to another. The reversible piecing technique would introduce a 1" straight edge between two scallops. I avoided this by using a version of a Hong Kong finish on the seam. To begin, cut a 1½" × 14" binding strip. Fold and press down 1" at one short end. Fold the quilted strip, right sides together, to form a tube. Pin the binding strip to one side of the lining, RST, with the folded edge at the top of the scallop panel. Sew through all the layers with a ½" seam allowance (Figure 2).

Press the seam allowances to one side. Press a ½" fold on the long side of the binding strip. Pin (from the right side) the binding strip over the seam allowance (Figure 3). Topstitch from the bag front.

Each side panel consists of one scallop. Insert a pin at each corner of the bag, placing the bound seam at one corner. Match the pins to the corners of the bag bottom rectangle (Figure 4). Sew the bottom to the bag, right sides together, with a ½" seam allowance. Serge the raw edges.

Press and turn the tote right side out. Press again. Folding the seamline with wrong sides together, edgestitch along all four edges at the bottom to give the bag a firm bottom. Pinching a vertical line with wrong sides together, edgestitch from each corner to the scallop top to create the boxy bottom shape of the bag.

Cut four 4" lengths of ribbon. Slip one handle ring onto each ribbon. Sew the ribbons to the bag.

Assemble the Tote, Figure 1

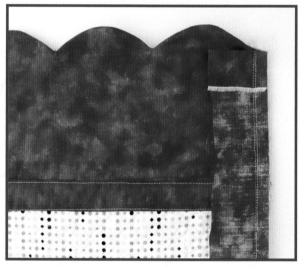

Assemble the Tote, Figure 2

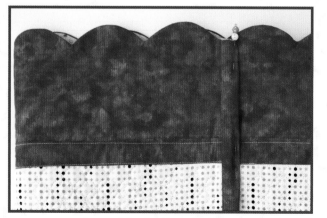

Assemble the Tote, Figure 3

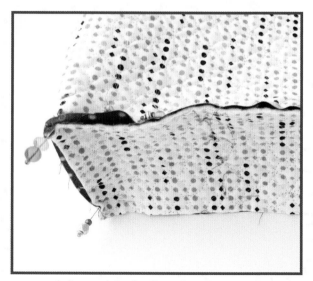

Assemble the Tote, Figure 4

My Favorite Bag

FINISHED SIZE: 12¾" × 12¾" × 3" (EXCLUDING HANDLES)

This project uses the following files: Swirl TopF1, Swirl BottomF1, DiamondNarrowBorderF2, CircleGrommetF1, Cool FlowerF2

The front and back of this bag consist of pieced sections with two different continuous embroidery designs. The top border incorporates more embroidery, a bit of appliqué, and grommets for a sturdy handle as well. This bag has a very complex look, but it isn't as difficult to make as it may appear.

STITCH PIECES FOR THE BAG BODY

Cut a 15" × WOF strip of base fabric. Layer this strip with batting and backing (the backing fabric will be visible on the inside of the bag). Six swirl sections will be stitched on this quilt sandwich. Hoop the upper left corner of the quilt sandwich. Select the Swirl TopF1 design. Embroider color 1, the alignment marks, and color 2 (Figure 1).

Carefully lift the top frame of the hoop and slide the fabric up to capture the bottom of the stitched design in the upper portion of the sewing field. Select the Swirl BottomF1 design and advance to the first stitch. The needle should be centered directly over the left alignment mark. Continue to advance through the stitches, watching the needle as it travels across the alignment mark. Use the flywheel to manually drop the needle to make sure the designs will connect (Figure 2). Advance through the stitches as the needle travels to the right alignment mark. It's not necessary to actually stitch the alignment marks. You can verify placement by watching the hoop move as you travel through the stitches.

Stitch the Swirl BottomF1 design. The top and bottom swirl designs make one section of the bag. Lift the top frame of the hoop and slide the fabric over to the left. Leave at least 1½" between the right edge of the first stitched section and the left edge of the next section. Stitch a total of six swirl sections, top and bottom.

Eileen tastefully used tonal background fabric and thread to create this classy bag. On my to-do list is to create this bag using a camel-colored linen fabric with black stitching. Just think of the options!

NOTES FROM NANCY

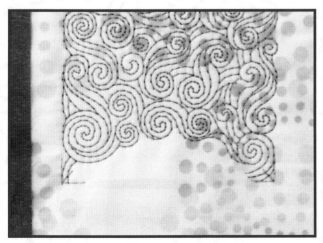

Stitch Pieces for the Bag Body, Figure 1

Stitch Pieces for the Bag Body, Figure 2

79

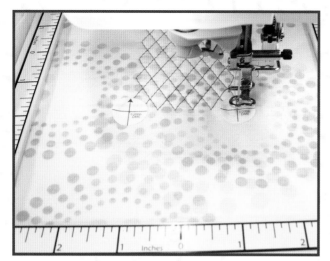

Stitch Pieces for the Bag Body, Figure 3

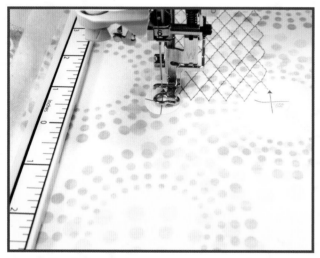

Stitch Pieces for the Bag Body, Figure 4

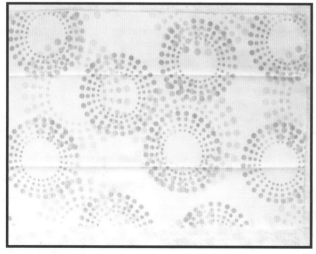

Stitch Pieces for the Bag Top, Figure 1

Cut a 15" × WOF strip of base fabric. Layer it with batting and backing fabric (this will be visible on the inside of the bag). Hoop the upper left portion of the fabric. Stitch the DiamondNarrowBorderF2 design. When the design is complete, use the trace feature to position the needle at the bottom left corner of the design. Place a target sticker directly under the needle. Move the needle to the bottom right corner and place another target sticker directly under the needle (Figure 3).

Carefully lift the top frame of the hoop and slide the fabric. Don't dislodge the target stickers while moving the fabric. Use the trace feature to position the needle at the top left corner of the design. Place the needle directly over the target sticker (Figure 4). Move the needle to the top right corner and place it directly over target sticker. Use the flywheel to manually drop the needle. The needle should pierce the target sticker in the center of each crosshair. If it doesn't, use one of the following methods to position the needle: use the jog keys to move the hoop, reposition the fabric by gently tugging on the fabric, or lift the hoop's top frame and move the fabric or rehoop.

If you would like one more reference point to double-check your placement, advance through the design to stitch 176. The needle will be positioned at the top of a diamond and should connect with the previously stitched design.

Remove the target stickers and embroider the DiamondNarrowBorderF2 design—one full diamond panel has been created. Repeat this process for a total of four full diamond panels, each at least 1½" away from those next to it. Trim the diamond panels leaving ½" of fabric beyond the stitching on each side. The remaining quilt sandwich should measure at least 15" × 30". Use this quilt sandwich to stitch the top borders.

STITCH PIECES FOR THE BAG TOP

Place the remaining quilt sandwich on a pressing surface with the long edges horizontal. Fold the bottom and top edge of the quilt sandwich into the middle and press the folds. Open the folds and smooth the quilt sandwich (Figure 1). Use the top and bottom creases as the horizontal center of each horizontal border. Two borders will fit on this quilt sandwich.

80

Hoop the left side of the quilt sandwich, centering the top crease in the hoop. Stitch one DiamondNarrow BorderF2 design (Figure 2). Lift the frame and slide the fabric to the left, then select the CircleGrommetF1 design. Use a ruler to allow ½" between the outer edges of the diamond grid and the grommet frame. Make sure the crease is still centered under the needle. Stitch the CircleGrommetF1 design (Figure 3).

Select the Cool FlowerF2 design. Slide the fabric to the left, leaving 1" between the outer edges of the grommet frame and the cool flower. Stitch colors 1 and 2 of the Cool FlowerF2 design. Place appliqué fabric over the design area and stitch color 3, the tackdown. Place a small piece of appliqué fabric over the center of the flower and stitch color 4 (Figure 4). Keeping the quilt sandwich in the hoop, trim the fabric from the flower to allow the next piece of appliqué to be stitched. Place a square of appliqué fabric over the flower and stitch colors 5 and 6.

Select the CircleGrommetF1 design. Slide the fabric to the left, leaving a 1" space between the outer edges of the cool flower and the grommet frame. Stitch the CircleGrommetF1 design. Select the DiamondNarrow BorderF2 design. Slide the fabric to the left ½". Stitch the DiamondNarrowBorderF2 design. Reposition the quilt sandwich to center the bottom crease in the hoop. Stitch a second top border to match the first.

TRIM THE PIECES

For each of the swirl and diamond sections, place the ½" mark of a quilter's ruler on the edges of the embroidered quilting designs and trim the excess fabric and batting (Figure 1). On the top borders, place the ½" mark of a quilter's ruler on the top edge of the flower design. Trim the excess fabric and batting. Repeat on the lower edge. The length of the top borders will be trimmed after piecing the bag body.

NOTES FROM **NANCY**

Computerized embroidery is not limited to a pretty design! If you have other bag or tote patterns with grommets, consider using a target sticker and embroidering this grommet placement embroidery. These embroideries are very versatile!

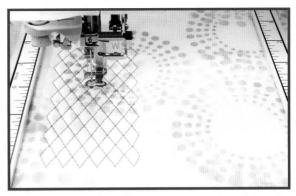

Stitch Pieces for the Bag Top, Figure 2

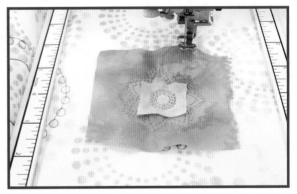

Stitch Pieces for the Bag Top, Figure 3

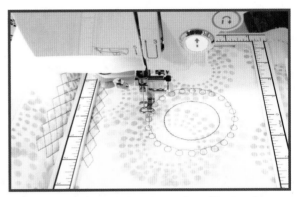

Stitch Pieces for the Bag Top, Figure 4

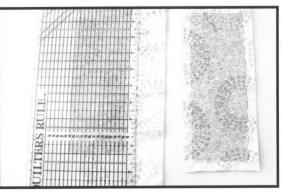

Trim the Pieces, Figure 1

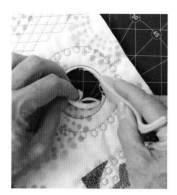

The Right Tool for the Job

There's a great little rotary cutter that does a fine job of slicing open the circles in this bag—the Fingertip Mini Rotary Cutter from Fiskars. It has a guide for your index finger and it allows you to cut any direction you please. It takes a minute or two to get used to, but it's ideal for going around tight curves – like these 2" circles!

Add the Grommets, Figure 1A

Add the Grommets, Figure 1B

ADD THE GROMMETS

Place a top border strip on a cutting mat. Slice away the fabric from the inner circle. Cut close to the stitching (Figures 1A and 1B).

Open the grommets; they have two sides, one male and one female. Insert the male grommet from the wrong side of the fabric (Figure 2). Place the female side on top and press the pieces together (Figure 3). Repeat for each grommet design.

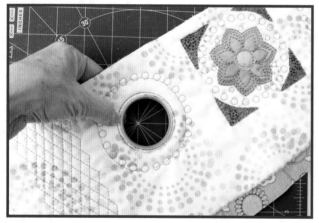

Add the Grommets, Figure 2

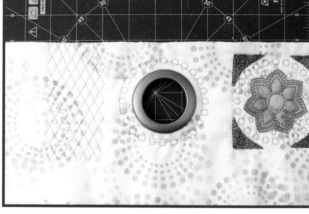

Add the Grommets, Figure 3

ASSEMBLE THE BAG

Cut sixteen 2" × 10" front and back sashing strips. Piece the bag front sections (three swirl sections and two diamond sections) together using reversible piecing (see pages 36–39). Repeat for the bag back.

Cut four 2" × 22½" front and back sashing strips. Center a top border on the bag front and piece the two together using reversible piecing (Figure 1). Repeat for the bag back. Trim the top borders even with the sides of the bag front and back.

Assemble the Bag, Figure 1

Measure and mark 2" in from each side at the top of the bag. Place a quilter's ruler on the bag, aligning the edge of the ruler with the 2" mark and the lower corner (Figure 2). Mark and cut on the line. Repeat for both sides of the bag top and bag bottom (Figure 3).

Cut one 2" × 22" front and back sashing strip. Piece the bag front to the bag back at the bottom with reversible piecing (Figure 4).

Cut four 2" × 13" front and back sashing strips. Make a double fold at one short end of each front and back sashing strip. Topstitch to finish the end. Use reversible piecing to attach the sides of the bag (Figure 5). Stitch the bottom of the sashing to the bottom of the bag.

Cut a 2" × 30" strip of sashing fabric to finish the upper edge. Press a ½" fold on one long side of the strip. Sew the short ends of the strip together to form a tube. Pin the tube, RST, to the bag front (Figure 6). Sew with a ½" seam allowance. Fold the strip over the top of the bag to the inside. Press, pin and topstitch from the front to secure.

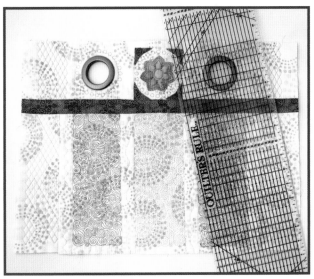

Assemble the Bag, Figure 2

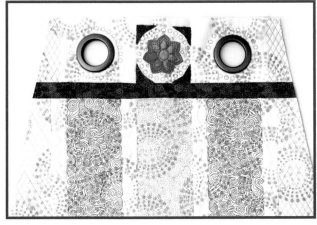

Assemble the Bag, Figure 3

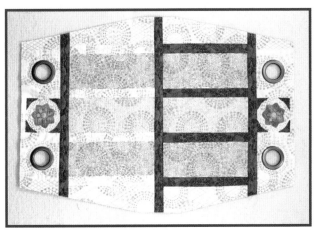

Assemble the Bag, Figure 4

Assemble the Bag, Figure 5

Assemble the Bag, Figure 6

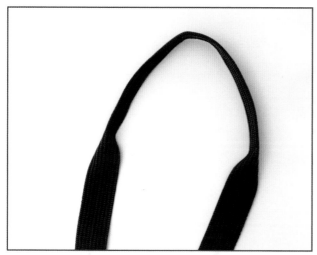
Create the Handles, Figure 1

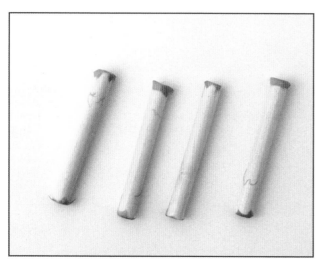
Create the Handles, Figure 2

CREATE THE HANDLES

Cut two 18" lengths of webbing. If the material is nylon, hold the cut edge over an open flame to singe and meld the fibers. Repeat for all four cut edges.

Fold the handle material in half lengthwise on a 10" section in the middle of the 18" length. Stitch along both sides of the 10" length (Figure 1). Repeat for the other strap.

Cut the 12" wood dowel into four 3" lengths. You can paint the handles to decorate them, or you can decoupage fabric onto the wood. If you choose to decoupage the handles, use Mod Podge to adhere fabric to the wood. This is best done in multiple layers over the course of a few days so the glue can dry properly. Apply fabric to the ends of the dowel first (Figure 2). After the ends are complete, roll a small fabric strip over the dowel. Sand and reapply Mod Podge as needed.

Place a 1" length of double-sided tape 2¼" from the end of the webbing on the wrong side of the material. Remove the protective covering from the tape. Center the dowel on the tape (Figure 3).

Wrap the end of the webbing over the dowel. Use a zipper foot to stitch the material as close as possible to the dowel.

Fold under the raw edge of the webbing and sew again (Figure 4). Repeat for all four dowels.

Insert the dowels into the grommets from the inside of the bag to the outside. The dowels will stop the straps from slipping through the grommets and add another decorative element to the bag.

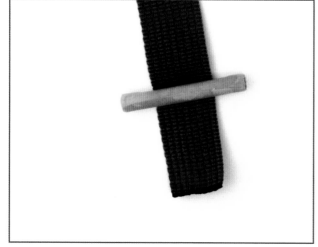
Create the Handles, Figure 3

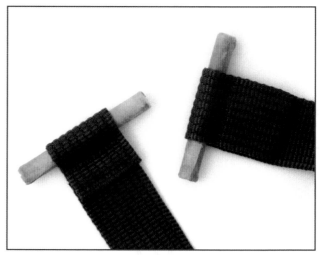
Create the Handles, Figure 4

Sewing Notions Caddy

FINISHED SIZE: 7½" TALL × 6¾" DIAMETER

This project uses the following files: Diamond GridF2, Floral SwagF2
How sweet is this handy organizer? Who would guess its humble beginnings of storing coffee? Now it's a darling addition to any embroidery studio. The scalloped border is simple to do with an embroidery machine, and because it's a digital file, the scallops will be perfect. Some savvy pressing lets the scallop facing do double duty as a decorative edge.

MAKE THE CADDY BASES

Make two 26" × 9" quilt sandwiches from the paisley fabric, batting and backing fabric; one sandwich is for the outside caddy base, and one is for the caddy base lining. Hoop the top left end of one quilt sandwich. Stitch the Diamond GridF2 design. When the design is complete, use the trace feature to position the needle at the bottom left corner of the design. Place a target sticker directly under the needle. Move the needle to the bottom right corner and place another target sticker directly under the needle (Figure 1).

Carefully lift the top frame of the hoop and slide the fabric in the hoop or rehoop the fabric without dislodging the target stickers. Use the trace feature to position the needle at what is now the top left corner of the design. Place the needle directly over the target sticker. Move the needle to the top right corner and place it directly over target sticker (Figure 2). Use the flywheel to manually drop the needle. The needle should pierce the target sticker in the center of each crosshair. If it does not, use one of the following methods to position the needle: use the jog keys to move the hoop, reposition the fabric by gently tugging on the fabric, or lift the hoop's top frame and move the fabric or rehoop.

If you would like one more reference point to double-check your placement, advance through the design to stitch 174. The needle will be positioned at the top of a diamond and should connect with the previously stitched design. Remove the target stickers and embroider the next Diamond GridF2 design. Stitch three repeats of Diamond GridF2 on each quilt sandwich.

Be sure to check out the DVD and click on *Continuous Applique* to see Eileen demonstrate this *Sewing Notions Caddy*. It's a clever concept and project!

NOTES FROM NANCY

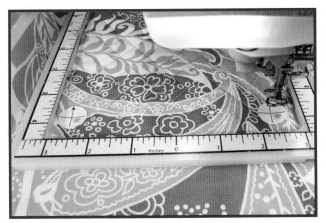
Make the Caddy Bases, Figure 1

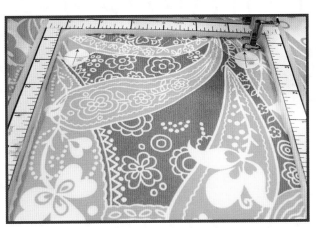
Make the Caddy Bases, Figure 2

Stitch the Floral Swag, Figure 1

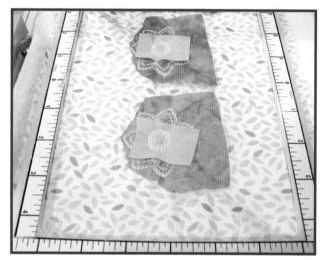

Stitch the Floral Swag, Figure 2

STITCH THE FLORAL SWAG

Cut six 3" squares of the coordinating semi-solid fabrics. Cut the yellow fabric into six 1" squares.

Make a 26" × 9" quilt cracker of the print fabric and batting. Hoop the left end of the strip. Stitch the Floral SwagF2 design starting with color 1, the stipple stitches, and color 2, the outline of the first flower. Place a square of appliqué fabric over the flower outline. Stitch color 3, the flower tackdown and petal details.

Stitch color 4, the outline of the second flower; after color 4 is complete, place a square of appliqué fabric over the flower outline. Stitch color 5, the flower tackdown and petal details (Figure 1).

Place a yellow square over the center of the second flower and stitch color 6, the flower center tackdown and details. After completing color 6, place a yellow fabric square over the center of the first flower and stitch color 7, the tackdown and details (Figure 2). Trim the lower edges of the flower appliqué fabrics so they don't extend beyond the stipple stitches.

Lay the top edge of a 26" × 5" strip of pink lining fabric over the design, right side down. Make sure ½" extends beyond the scallop-shaped side (Figure 3). Stitch color 8, the scallop outline.

Lift the appliqué fabric back over the design. Use the trace feature to position the needle over the lower left corner of the design. Place a target sticker under the needle. Position the needle over the lower right corner of the design and place a target sticker under the needle (Figure 4).

Stitch the Floral Swag, Figure 3

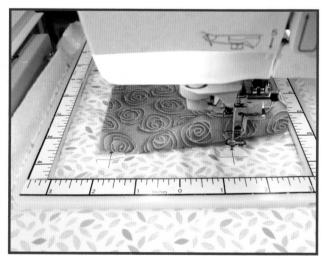

Stitch the Floral Swag, Figure 4

Carefully lift the top frame of the hoop and slide the fabric or rehoop the fabric. Don't dislodge the target stickers while moving the fabric. Use the trace feature to position the needle at the top left corner of the design. Place the needle directly over the target sticker. Move the needle to the top right corner and place it directly over the target sticker. Use the flywheel to manually drop the needle. The needle should pierce the target sticker in the center of each crosshair.

Stitch the next set of appliqués. Keep the pink appliqué fabric out of the design area during the first seven colors (Figures 5 and 6). Smooth the appliqué fabric into place and stitch color 8. Repeat the process once more and remove the strip from the hoop. The floral swag will have a total of six flowers.

TRIM AND ASSEMBLE PIECES

Measure the circumference and height of the container you're using for your caddy. Trim the caddy base strip ½" from one long edge of the quilting. Trim the opposite side so the strip measures the height of the can plus ½" for ease (Figure 1).

Cut a front and back sashing strip 2" wide by the height of the trimmed caddy base strip. Consider using the same fabric as the caddy base for an inconspicuous finish. Sew the short ends of the caddy base together using reversible piecing (see pages 36–39). Stitch in the ditch on the sashing (Figure 2).

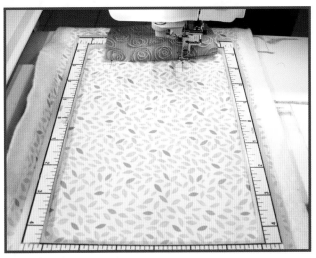

Stitch the Floral Swag, Figure 5

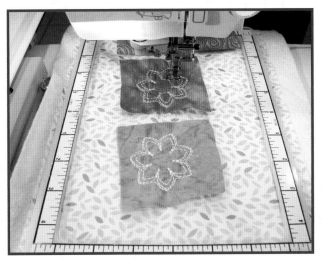

Stitch the Floral Swag, Figure 6

Trim and Assemble Pieces, Figure 1

Trim and Assemble Pieces, Figure 2

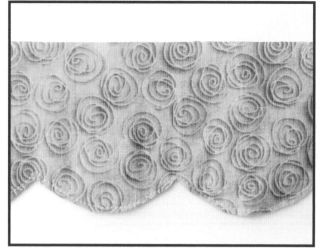

Trim and Assemble Pieces, Figure 3

Trim and Assemble Pieces, Figure 4

Baste the upper edge of the quilted strip since the quilting does not extend all the way to the edge.

Trim the scalloped edge of the floral swag strip approximately ⅛" from the stitching. Clip around the scallops and into the peak of each scallop, being careful not to clip the stitches. Trim the border so it measures 4" from the top cut edge to the bottom of the finished scallops (Figure 3). Cut the length to the can circumference plus ½" for ease.

Turn the floral swag right side out using a point turner. Carefully insert the point turner into each curved scallop and smooth the seam. Allow an even amount of facing fabric to peek out from the back (Figure 4).

Cut one 2"× 6" front and back sashing strip. Sew the floral swag strip into a tube using reversible piecing. When adding the front and back sashing, make sure the sashing ends extend about 1" below the strip. Trim and stitch the excess fabric of the sashing to follow the lines of the scallop pattern (Figure 5).

Slide the outer caddy base tube over the can, right side out. Slide the floral swag tube, right side out, over the quilted strip. Align the seams and top edges. Pin the two pieces together (Figure 6). Remove the fabrics from the can and baste the layers together.

Cut one 24" length of 1⅞"-wide bias strip (this includes a ½" seam allowance) from one of the semi-solid fabrics. Wrap the bias strip around the fusible piping, centering the piping in the fold. Press with a dry iron in the seam allowance only. Do not fuse the last 4" of the bias strip.

Trim and Assemble Pieces, Figure 5

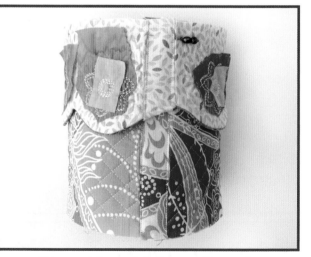

Trim and Assemble Pieces, Figure 6

Starting with the unfused end, align the raw edge of the cord with the raw edge of the pinned caddy base and swag. Attach a zipper foot to your sewing machine. Start sewing 2" from the fused end and continue around the tube.

To finish the ends of the cord, butt the ends of the cord together. Peel back the fabric to expose the cord and snip the cord where the two ends meet (Figure 7).

Fold the edge of the bias strip and finger press. Insert the other end of the cord into the bias strip, covering the end of the cord with the fabric. Pin in the seam allowance and stitch to secure (Figure 8). Add binding around the bottom of the caddy base using a traditional method or the super-fast, fusible binding method (see page 40).

Insert the second caddy base strip inside the container. Mark the strip for finished length and height; to the height, add ¾" (½" for the top seam allowance and ¼" for the bottom seam allowance). Trim at the marks. Cut a front and back sashing strip 2" wide by the height of the trimmed caddy base lining strip. Sew the short ends of the caddy base lining strip together with reversible piecing to create a tube. Mark the tube in quarters.

Trace the bottom of the can on the lining fabric. Cut out the circle, adding a ¼" seam allowance. Mark the circle in quarters. Pin the circle to the caddy base lining strip, right sides together, matching all quarter marks. Sew with a ¼" seam allowance.

Insert the cover into the lining, right sides together. Sew with a ½" seam allowance at the top edge. Trim the seam allowance. Turn and press right side out. Place the finished caddy cover over the can (Figure 9).

Trim and Assemble Pieces, Figure 7

Trim and Assemble Pieces, Figure 8

Trim and Assemble Pieces, Figure 9

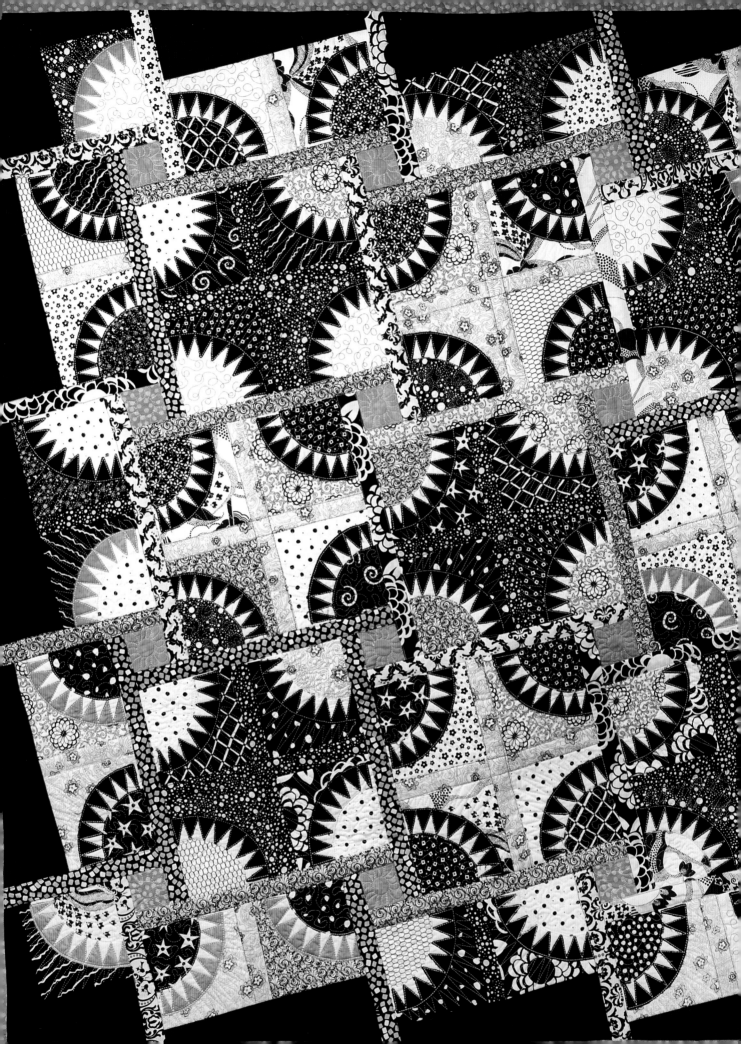

CHAPTER 7

Quilts

All my sewing life, I've loved quilting. All my sewing life, I've struggled with quilting. I'm not a perfectionist, so I often move too quickly through tasks, and then I'm disappointed with the results. I've learned there are some things I'm capable of changing—other things, not so much!

I know I can't change my approach to sewing tasks, but I can change the technique. The revolutionary techniques in this book get me the finish I seek without the tedious, meticulous cutting and piecing that I don't have the patience to endure. For heaven's sake, I'm getting older—I'm running out of time, my hands hurt and my eyes are fading. These are facts that I can't change, but I can use techniques, and tools, that are friendlier to me, and you can do the same. Drop your quilting guard and look at these quilts with a respect for the technique and finished results. And the bonus is they can be completed in manageable sections of both fabric and time!

Each block in the *Ohio Star Quilt* on page 94 takes under 10 minutes to stitch, so it's realistic to stitch six blocks in 90 minutes. Because all trimming is done once the blocks are removed from the hoop, you can trim at your leisure—in front of the television if you'd like. Remember to select contrasting fabrics to let the stars pop. Experiment with different color combinations until you find your favorite.

I am quite proud of the *Lady Liberty Quilt* on page 100. The colors are striking, as are the points of the lady's crown. The border was enhanced by the inclusion of half-circle sections—you can opt to include them or not. Make the quilt your own by adding an interesting layout of the blocks and borders.

The *New York Beauty Quilt* on page 110 was inspired by a quilt I saw in a quilting magazine many years ago. I was always mesmerized by the layout of the blocks. It's a challenge, but one you'll get the hang of as you proceed through the piecing. It's worth it—you'll be proud of yourself when it's finished!

Basket of Blooms on page 116 is a two-hoop large appliqué. The upper portion of the block (most of the stems and flowers) is stitched first. Then the bottoms of the stems are hidden by the basket. This block would look great in a four- or eight-block quilt. Just switch out the fabrics for each block to add variety. The vertical and horizontal borders are quite fun—three hoopings make these borders appear to be seamless. Follow the directions to stitch the sections in the proper order because some of the appliqués are strategically placed to hide other elements.

Let the techniques in this book revolutionize your quilting!

Ohio Star Quilt

FINISHED SIZE: 37" × 37"

This project uses the following files: OhioStarNoSqF1, OhStDiamondBlkF1, Ohio Star CornerF1, Ohio BorderF1

This quilt mixes two techniques: appliquéd blocks and continuous appliquéd strips. The quilt blocks are very easy and can be produced in a flash. The continuous appliqué looks complicated, but a few insider tips make this technique a winner for embroiderers of all skill levels. The designs on the star blocks showcase the stitches, not the fabrics, so work with plain fabrics and contrasting threads to show off the tiny stitches and elegant feathers.

GATHER THESE ITEMS

White fabric: ¾ yd.

Black fabric: ½ yd.

Blue fabric: ⅞ yd.

Print fabric: ⅔ yd.

Yellow fabric: 1⅛ yds.

Backing fabric: 2 yds.

Batting: 73" × 45"

5" × 7" hoop

MAKE THE OHIO STAR BLOCKS

This quilt requires fourteen Ohio Star blocks: five with black appliqué and nine with blue appliqué.

From the white fabric, cut a 9" strip × WOF and layer it with batting and backing. You will stitch 5" blocks on this strip, each separated by 1½", so you will need a total of three quilt sandwiches.

Hoop one end of the quilt sandwich. Stitch OhioStarNoSqF1 starting with color 1, the stipple (Figure 1). Place a 5½" square of appliqué fabric (either blue or black, to match the thread color of the stippling) over the stipple. Sew color 2, the appliqué tackdown (Figure 2). Finally, sew color 3, the feather decoration on the star (Figure 3). Remove the top frame of the hoop and slide the fabric up to encase a new design area. Use your machine's trace feature to locate the top of the design. Make sure there is at least 1½" between the bottom of the first design and the top of the second design. Repeat these steps to make all of the Ohio Star blocks.

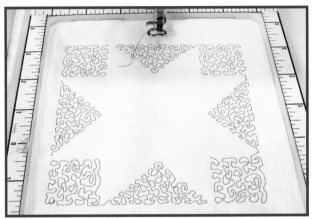

Make the Ohio Star Blocks, Figure 1

The Ohio Star is a classic patchwork design. Consider creating it with thread only! Instead of adding the applique fabric, experiment with three different thread colors, stitching on a solid fabric background.

NOTES FROM **NANCY**

Make the Ohio Star Blocks, Figure 2

Make the Ohio Star Blocks, Figure 3

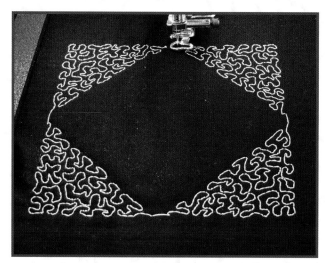

Create the Diamond Blocks, Figure 1

Create the Diamond Blocks, Figure 2

CREATE THE DIAMOND BLOCKS

You will also need to create eleven diamond blocks for this quilt: six black blocks and five blue blocks.

Cut a 9" strip × WOF from the blue fabric and the black fabric. Layer these strips with batting and backing to make two quilt sandwiches. You will stitch 5" blocks on these strips, each separated by 1½".

Stitch OhStDiamondBlkF1 starting with color 1, the stipple (Figure 1). Place a 5½" square of appliqué fabric (the print fabric) over the stipple.

Sew color 2, the appliqué tackdown, and then color 3, the feather decoration on the diamond (Figure 2). Remove the top frame of the hoop and slide the fabric up to encase a new design area. Use your machine's trace feature to locate the top of the design. Make sure there is at least 1½" between the bottom of the first design and the top of the second design. Repeat these steps to make all of the diamond blocks.

FINISHING THE BLOCKS

Once all the embroidery is complete, trim away the excess appliqué fabric (see page 23) (Figure 1). Square the blocks to 6" (Figure 2). To do this, place the ½" mark of a quilter's ruler on the embroidered edge of the block and trim the excess fabric. Repeat for all four sides. When trimming between two blocks, be aware of the seam allowance on both blocks. If the blocks are very close (less than 1½") use caution when trimming because the embroidery may not be perfectly square.

Arrange the trimmed blocks on a design wall until you find a layout you like. Shoot a digital image of the layout to use as a guide during the piecing process.

Finishing the Blocks, Figure 1

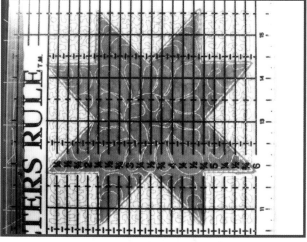

Finishing the Blocks, Figure 2

STITCH THE BORDERS

For this project, you will need to create four border strips. I usually piece all blocks before beginning the border. This gives me the freedom to audition different fabrics, colors and border layouts. Whatever design process you choose, use the design wall to keep everything in order.

Cut a 9" × 35" strip of yellow fabric and layer it with batting and backing. You will stitch two Ohio BorderF1 designs (2½" × 30") separated by 1½" on this strip. The border is stitched from left to right. Hoop the left end of the yellow strip. Stitch color 1, the stipple.

Cut a 3" × 34" strip of printed fabric. Place the appliqué strip over the design area. Make sure the width of the strip spans the entire stippled area. Stitch color 2, the tackdown. Next, stitch color 3, the feather quilting.

Lift the strip of appliqué fabric back over the design (Figure 1). Use the trace feature to position the needle at the bottom left corner of the design. Place a target sticker directly under the needle. Move the needle to the bottom right corner and place a target sticker directly under the needle (Figure 2).

Carefully lift the top frame of the hoop and slide the fabric up so the next design area is in the hoop. Don't dislodge the target stickers while moving the fabric and keep the appliqué strip out of the hoop. Once the backing, batting and yellow fabric are re-hooped, fold the appliqué strip back over the previously embroidered design and out of the way. Use the trace feature to position the needle at the top left corner of the design. Place the needle directly over the target sticker (Figure 3). Move the needle to the top right corner and place it directly over the target sticker. Use the flywheel to manually drop the needle. The needle should pierce the target sticker in the center of the crosshair. If the needle doesn't hit the center of the target sticker, use one of the following methods to position the needle: use the jog keys to move the hoop, reposition the fabric by gently tugging on the fabric or lift the hoop's the top frame and move the fabric or rehoop.

Remove the target stickers and embroider the next portion of the design, smoothing the print fabric into position for color 2. Stitch six repeats of Ohio BorderF1 and then repeat on the right-hand side of the quilt sandwich. Repeat once more on a second quilt sandwich for a total of four borders.

Stitch the Borders, Figure 1

In the photos on this page, one border is already complete, and I am stitching the second border on the piece of yellow fabric.

When Eileen and I filmed the enclosed DVD, it was the first time that I used the Snap-Hoop. This is the classic case of using the right tool to achieve the best result.

NOTES FROM NANCY

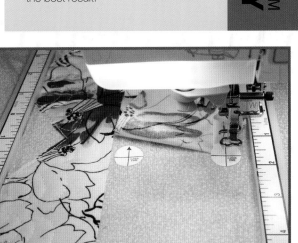

Stitch the Borders, Figure 2

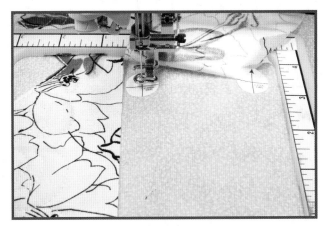

Stitch the Borders, Figure 3

CREATE THE CORNERSTONES

This design includes four quilted cornerstones with no appliqué. To stitch the Ohio Star CornerF1 design, hoop one 10" × 12" piece of yellow fabric with batting and backing. Stitch four Ohio Star CornerF1 designs, spacing them at least 1½" apart (Figure 1). Cut the corner designs to measure 4" × 4"—this creates four 3" blocks with ½" seam allowances on all four sides.

PIECE THE QUILT

Cut twenty front vertical sashing strips (2" × 6") from the yellow fabric and twenty back vertical sashing strips (2" × 6") from the backing fabric.

Use reversible piecing (see pages 36–39) and ½" seam allowances to assemble two blocks (Figure 1). Repeat the process to piece five blocks to make one row. Repeat for five rows. As you make the rows, mark the first block on the left side to designate both its row number and orientation. Marking all five rows in the same manner will help you piece the rows later.

Next, cut twenty front horizontal sashing strips (2" × 6") from the yellow fabric and sixteen sashing cornerstones (2" × 2") from the blue fabric. Piece the sashing strips to the cornerstones using ½" seam allowances (Figure 2). Press the seam allowances toward the darker fabric. The finished horizontal pieced sashing strips will measure 30" × 2". Make four. Cut four 30" × 2" sashing strips from the backing fabric.

Add the pieced horizontal sashings to the bottom of each horizontal row of blocks along with the back sashing. Sew the rows together using reversible piecing.

PIECE THE BORDERS

Piece the vertical borders using reversible piecing in this order: cornerstone, blue front and back sashing (3½" × 2"), vertical border, blue front and back sashing, cornerstone. Make two.

Cut two 30" × 2" strips each of blue fabric and backing fabric. Piece the blue sashing strips and back sashing strips to the top and bottom of the quilt. Press the front sashings open. Sew the horizontal borders to the sashing using reversible piecing.

Cut two 37" × 2" blue vertical sashing strips (front and back) and piece them to the vertical edges of the quilt. Sew the vertical borders to the quilt.

Bind the quilt with blue fabric using a traditional method or the super-fast, fusible binding method (see page 40). Add a sleeve and label to the back of the quilt if you desire.

Create the Cornerstones, Figure 1

Piece the Quilt, Figure 1

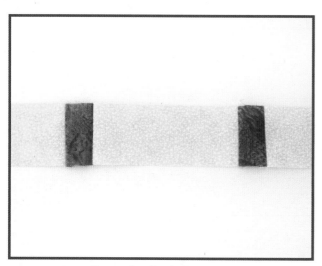

Piece the Quilt, Figure 2

99

Lady Liberty Quilt

FINISHED SIZE: 38½" × 27½"

This project uses the following files: LadyLibertyL6F2, LLCorner2F2, LL3 DiamondF1, LLBorder2F1, LLBorder6F1, LLMidBorderF2; a bonus design, LLl3F2, is also included on the DVD

I have always been intrigued by the Lady Liberty quilt block. I love the contrast of the light and dark values in the pointy spikes. However, I've always been petrified of tackling a Lady Liberty block in the traditional pieced or paper-pieced manner. Machine embroidery to the rescue! Now the points can be teeny-tiny and super-pointy because the digital file does all the work. I just lay the fabrics down in the right sequence and trim later. Give it a try. I think you'll be pleased with the results.

MAKE THE LADY LIBERTY BLOCKS

This quilt requires twenty-one LadyLibertyL6F2 blocks in assorted colors (you can substitute LLl3F2 blocks if you wish). The look of this quilt is all about contrast—the value of the base fabric should contrast with the value of each appliqué fabric. If you like your quilting stitches to be highly visible, select a contrasting thread for each color sequence as well.

To make the LadyLibertyL6F2 blocks, cut a 9" × WOF strip from each of your six base fabrics. Make a quilt sandwich with batting and backing on each.

Hoop one end of a quilt sandwich. Stitch LadyLibertyL6F2 starting with color 1, the decorative quilting stitches, on the block fabric (Figure 1). After completing color 1, lay a piece of appliqué fabric at least 5" square on the block for the spikes. Stitch color 2, the outline of the quarter circle, and color 3, the tackdown of the spikes (Figure 2).

GATHER THESE ITEMS

Quilt block base fabric: ¼ yd. each of 6 different fabrics (dark blue, medium blue, lime green, bright orange, bright green and aqua)

Quilt block appliqué fabric: minimum ¾ yd. of assorted fabrics, at least a fat eighth of each; scrap fabrics are also great for this quilt, as long as they are pieces that are at least 5" square

Border base fabric: ⅞ yd.

Border appliqué fabric: ⅓ yd.

Border sashing: ⅛ yd.

Binding: ⅛ yd.

Backing fabric: 1½ yds.

Batting: 83" × 45"

5" × 7" hoop

Make the Lady Liberty Blocks, Figure 1

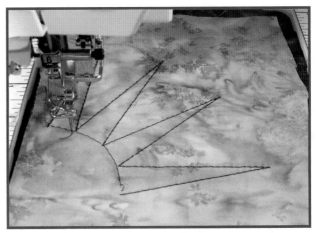

Make the Lady Liberty Blocks, Figure 2

101

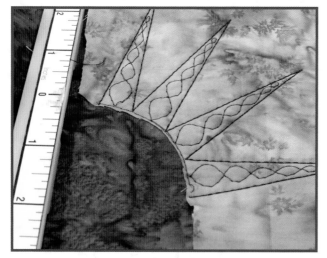

Make the Lady Liberty Blocks, Figure 3

Stitch color 4, the decorative quilting stitches on the spikes. After completing color 4, remove the hoop from the machine and carefully trim the fabric from inside the quarter circle (Figure 3).

Reattach the hoop to the machine. Lay a piece of appliqué fabric at least 3½" square over the opening in the block for the quarter circle (Figure 4). Make sure the appliqué fabric extends ½" into the seam allowance beyond the block dimensions.

Stitch color 5, the quarter circle tackdown and stipple. Lift the hoop frame and slide the fabric to position the next block in the hoop. Leave at least 1" between the blocks. Repeat for all twenty-one LadyLibertyL6F2 blocks.

After the blocks are complete, trim the appliqué fabrics. On the quarter circles, trim only the curved edge (Figure 5). Leave the excess appliqué fabric to extend into the seam allowance. On the spikes, hold your scissors very close to the stitched tackdown and cut away the excess fabric (Figure 6). This will help when piecing the blocks together. Trim all blocks to 5½" square (this includes a ¼" seam allowance on all sides).

Make the Lady Liberty Blocks, Figure 4

Take the time to make a test block before cutting all the fabric. This is a dramatic design that can be further enhanced with the right color fabric/thread choices. The test block could always become part of the label!

NOTES FROM NANCY

Make the Lady Liberty Blocks, Figure 5

Make the Lady Liberty Blocks, Figure 6

CREATE THE DIAMOND BLOCKS

This quilt also includes three LL3 DiamondF1 blocks. Use any leftover space on the quilt sandwiches you created for the LadyLibertyL6F2 blocks to stitch the diamond blocks using the LL3 DiamondF1 design.

To begin, stitch color 1, the stipple (Figure 1). After completing color 1, place a piece of appliqué fabric at least 3½" square over the outline and stitch color 2, the tackdown of the small triangles (Figure 2).

If you want to use two different appliqué fabrics on the block, remove the hoop from the machine after stitching color 2. Trim the excess appliqué fabric away from the small triangles (Figure 3).

Reattach the hoop to the machine and place a piece of appliqué fabric at least 5" square over the block (Figure 4). Stitch color 3, the diamond tackdown, and color 4, the inside detail on the diamonds (Figure 5).

After the blocks are complete, trim the appliqué fabrics. Trim all blocks to 5½" square (this includes a ¼" seam allowance on all sides).

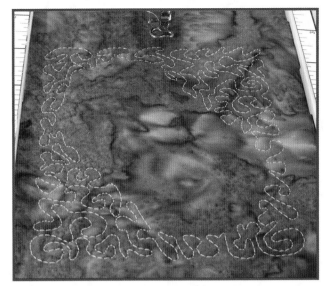

Create the Diamond Blocks, Figure 1

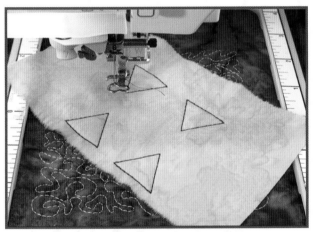

Create the Diamond Blocks, Figure 2

Create the Diamond Blocks, Figure 3

Create the Diamond Blocks, Figure 4

Create the Diamond Blocks, Figure 5

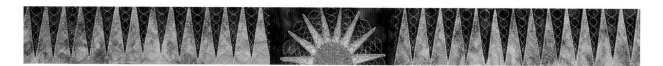

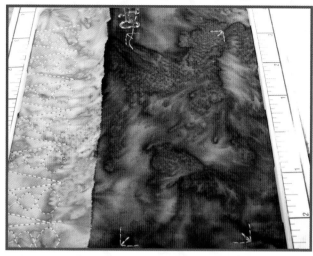

Stitch the Horizontal Borders, Figure 1

STITCH THE HORIZONTAL BORDERS

This quilt has two horizontal borders, each 2¾" × 33". To make a complete horizontal border, you'll need one mid-border design (LLMidBorderF2), plus two spike border strips. The spike border strips are composed of two six-spike stitched designs (LLBorder6F1) and one two-spike stitched design (LLBorder2F1) for a total of fourteen spikes on each side of the mid-border design.

To create the spike border strips, cut a 10" × WOF strip of border base fabric. Layer it with batting and backing. The spike border designs for both horizontal borders (a total of four) will be embroidered on this quilt sandwich. Chalk a vertical line 1½" from one long edge. Use this as an alignment guide for embroidering in a continuous line.

Hoop the left end of the quilt sandwich, placing the chalked line on the inside edge of the hoop. Stitch color 1 of LLBorder6F1, the alignment marks, on the base fabric (Figure 1). After the first color is complete, stitch color 2, the decorative loops (Figure 2).

Cut a 3" × WOF strip of the border appliqué fabric for the spikes. Place the appliqué fabric over the decorative loops. Make sure the width of the strip spans the entire design area. Stitch color 3, the spike tackdown. Stitch color 4, the decorative loops on the spikes (Figure 3).

Fold the appliqué strip back over the previously embroidered portion and on top of the hoop (Figure 4). Carefully lift the top frame of the hoop and slide the fabric up. Keep the appliqué strip out of the hoop.

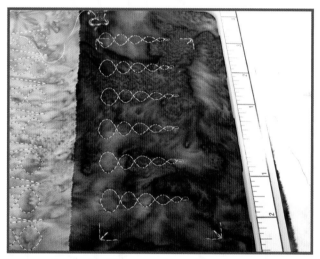

Stitch the Horizontal Borders, Figure 2

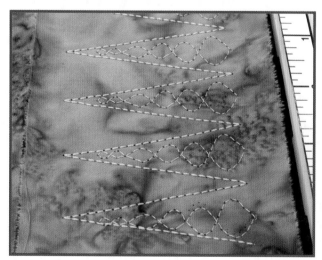

Stitch the Horizontal Borders, Figure 3

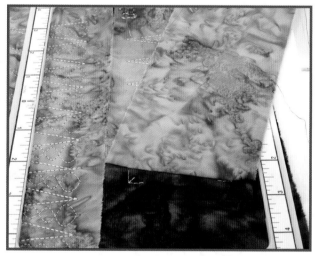

Stitch the Horizontal Borders, Figure 4

Use the trace feature on your embroidery machine to position the needle at what is now the top left corner of the design. Make sure the new LLBorder6F1 design is positioned directly below the previously stitched design. Advance to the first stitch, moving the hoop to the first stitch of the top left alignment mark (Figure 5). The needle should line up with the previous design's bottom alignment mark. Use the flywheel to manually drop the needle. The needle should pierce the alignment mark.

Advance through the design to position the needle over the top right alignment mark. It should align with the previous stitched alignment mark (Figure 6). If the needle doesn't align with the mark, use one of the following methods to position the needle: use the jog keys to move the hoop, reposition the fabric by gently tugging on the fabric or lift the hoop's top frame and move the fabric or rehoop.

Stitch colors 1 and 2, keeping the appliqué strip out of the design area (Figure 7). Smooth the appliqué fabric strip onto the design area after stitching colors 1 and 2 (Figure 8). Repeat to add the LLBorder2F1 design after the two six-spike designs are complete.

To stitch the second horizontal border, secure the upper right portion of the quilt sandwich strip in the hoop. Use the edge of the previously stitched border to square the fabric in the hoop. Use the trace feature and position the needle in the far left point of the design. Make sure this point is at least 1" from the previously stitched design. This will allow for ample seam allowance on each border. Stitch the second strip as you did the first. Repeat for the third and fourth strips.

After the spike border strips are complete, trim the appliqué fabric. Hold your scissors close to the stitched tackdown and cut away the excess fabric. With the spikes centered, trim each strip to 2¾" × 13¼".

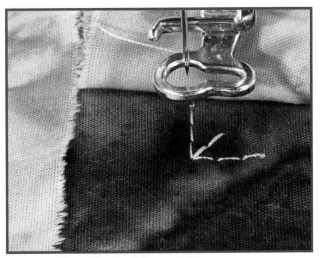

Stitch the Horizontal Borders, Figure 5

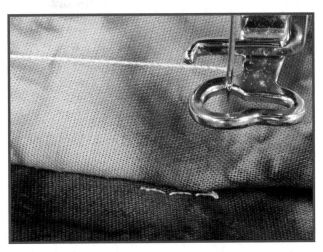

Stitch the Horizontal Borders, Figure 6

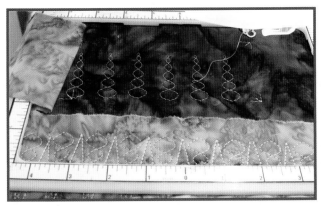

Stitch the Horizontal Borders, Figure 7

Stitch the Horizontal Borders, Figure 8

To make the mid-border pieces, hoop a 9" × 15" quilt sandwich of border base fabric, batting and backing. Stitch color 1, the quilted loops, on the base fabric (Figure 9).

Place the appliqué fabric for the spikes over the design area. Stitch color 2, the circle guide, and color 3, the spikes' tackdown. Stitch color 4, the decorative details on the spikes (Figure 10).

Remove the hoop from the machine and carefully trim the fabric away from the half circle and the two outside edges of the outside spikes (Figure 11). Place the sun appliqué fabric over the half circle and stitch color 5, the tackdown and stipple detail (Figure 12). Lift the hoop frame and slide the fabric to position the next block in the hoop. Leave at least 1" between the blocks.

After the blocks are complete, trim the appliqué fabrics. On the half circles, trim the curved edge. Leave the excess appliqué fabric to extend into the seam allowance. On the spikes, hold your scissors very close to the stitched tackdown and cut away the excess fabric. Centering the embroidery, trim the pieces to 2¾" × 6½".

The horizontal borders also include four corner units, which are created in the same manner as the mid-border units and have a finished size of 2¾" × 2¾". Stitch all four LLCorner2F2 units on one 10" × 10" quilt sandwich.

VERTICAL BORDERS

To make the vertical borders, follow the same steps as the horizontal borders to make two more mid-border pieces and four more spike border strips. The spike border strips for the vertical borders have one LLBorder6F1design and one LLBorder2F1 design. The finished size of the vertical borders is 2¾" × 22".

NOTES FROM **NANCY**

The mid-border embroidery could easily be used on a denim jacket. In my mind's eye, it could be placed at the center back of a yoke with the spiked designs stitched along the hem!

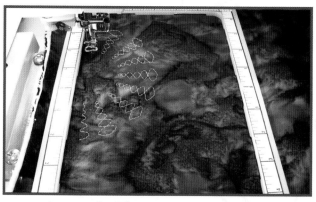

Stitch the Horizontal Borders, Figure 9

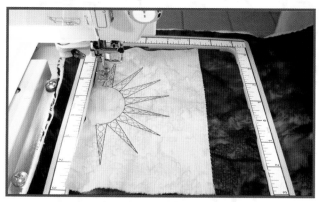

Stitch the Horizontal Borders, Figure 10

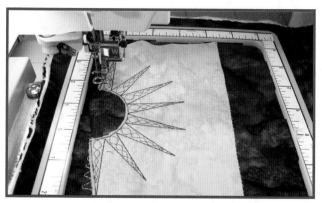

Stitch the Horizontal Borders, Figure 11

Stitch the Horizontal Borders, Figure 12

ASSEMBLE THE QUILT

All of the quilt components are now complete. Use a design wall to audition different layouts of the quilt blocks. Shoot digital images to record your changes, then review the images to determine what layout works best. Once you're satisfied with your decision, place the blocks in the proper order on the design wall. Or change it up again—my version changed many times! When it's time to piece the blocks into rows, take one row at a time to the sewing machine. Once the row is assembled, place the pieced row back on the wall to keep everything in order.

For this quilt, the finished width of all the sashing strips is ½". Normally, I like to work with a finished width of 1" (the quilter-friendly ½" seam allowances are so much easier to piece than traditional ¼" seam allowances), but the 1"-wide sashing overpowered the narrow spikes on each block.

To begin assembly, cut eighteen front vertical sashing strips (1" × 5½") from the leftover appliqué fabrics and eighteen back vertical sashing strips (1⅛" × 5½") from the backing fabric. This extra ⅛" on the back sashing makes catching the fold on the back so much easier when working with small seam allowances such as ¼".

Use reversible piecing and ¼" seam allowances (see pages 36–39) to assemble two blocks (Figures 1–3). If you are piecing two blocks with the suns rising in the same direction, use pins to join the blocks to form one continuous line (Figure 4). Piece four blocks to make one vertical row. Repeat for six rows.

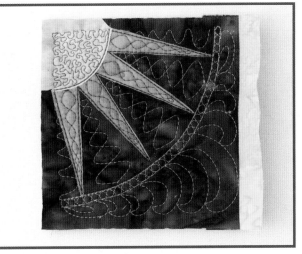

Assemble the Quilt, Figure 1

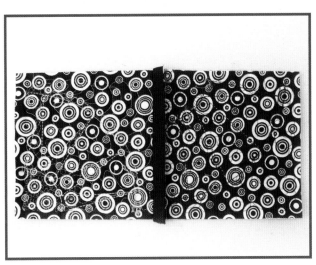

Assemble the Quilt, Figure 2

Assemble the Quilt, Figure 3

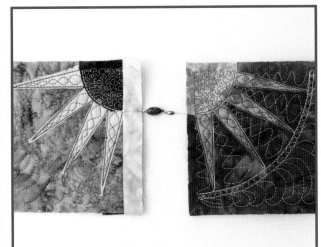

Assemble the Quilt, Figure 4

Assemble the Quilt, Figure 5

The vertical rows on this quilt are separated by pieced sashing that spans across one block and one sashing strip (see page 38). Make five 1" × 22" pieced sashing strips (Figure 5). Assemble the rows (Figures 6–8). Once all rows are pieced, add 1" × 22" vertical sashing (front and back) to the right and left sides of the quilt.

Piece the vertical borders: Attach one spike border strip to 1" × 2¾" sashing, add one mid-border piece, then 1" × 2¾" sashing and end with one spike border strip. Sew the vertical borders to the sides of the quilt, matching the center of the border to the center of the quilt.

Piece the horizontal borders: Attach one corner piece to 1" × 2¾" sashing, add one spike border strip and join 1" × 2¾" sashing. Next, attach one mid-border piece followed by 1" × 2¾" sashing, then one spike border strip, then 1" × 2¾" sashing and finally end with one corner piece.

Add 1" × 38½" horizontal sashing (front and back) to the top and bottom of the quilt. Attach the horizontal borders to the quilt. Match the center of the border to the center of the quilt.

Bind the quilt using a traditional method or the super-fast, fusible binding method (see page 40). Add a sleeve and label to the back of the quilt if you desire.

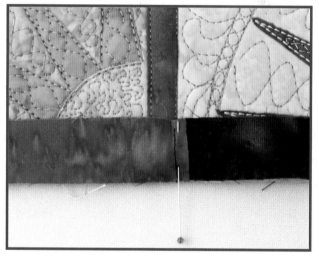

Assemble the Quilt, Figure 6

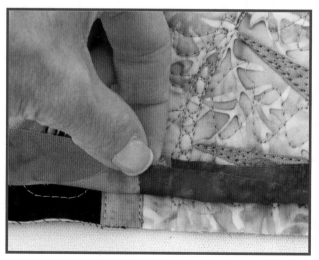

Assemble the Quilt, Figure 7

Assemble the Quilt, Figure 8

109

New York Beauty Quilt

FINISHED SIZE: 54" × 54"

This project uses the following files: NY Beauty, NY BeautyStipple, NY Setting Stone

I've always been drawn to black-and-white fabrics, and for this quilt I concentrated on how the value and the scale of these prints can impact a design. When selecting fabrics for each block, use opposite values for the inside and outside corners while paying special attention to the prints; try to incorporate two prints of varying scale into one block. You can use a value viewer to determine if a black-and-white print is a light- or a dark-value fabric.

I recommend not using this as your first project from this book—this quilt challenged me more than any project I've attempted in years. Making the blocks and the four-block units were a breeze, but when it came time to piece the units together with setting stones, I thought I was in over my head! But I plowed ahead, and I'm glad I did. This is the most accurate square quilt I've ever made, thanks to the digital files! This is a great quilt to try if you are up to a challenge.

GATHER THESE ITEMS

White fabric: 3 yds.

Black fabric: 1½ yds.

Pink fabric: ⅓ yd.

Aqua fabric: ⅓ yd.

Print fabric: 15 different black-and-white prints, one 14" × WOF strip of each

Binding fabric: ⅓ yd.

Backing fabric: 3 yds.

Batting: 162" × 45"

5" × 7" hoop

PREPARE TO SEW

Cut eleven 9" × WOF strips of white fabric, batting and backing and assemble these pieces into quilt sandwiches. Cut and separate the print fabrics into four piles: thirty-one 4" squares of light-value fabrics, thirty-two 6" squares of light-value fabrics, thirty-three 4" squares of dark-value fabrics and thirty-two 6" squares of dark-value fabrics.

STITCH LARGE BLOCKS

This quilt contains sixty-four NY Beauty blocks in a variety of color schemes. Make:

    26 dark blocks with black points
    6 dark blocks with pink points
    25 light blocks with black points
    7 light blocks with pink points

To make the dark blocks with black points, hoop one quilt sandwich. Stitch the NY Beauty design beginning with color 1 in white, the placement guide for both center curves (Figure 1). Place a 6" dark square on the outside right corner, covering the larger curve (Figure 2).

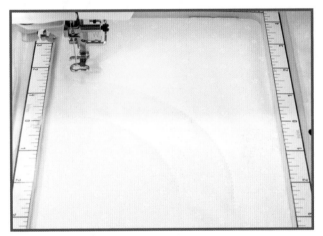

Stitch Large Blocks, Figure 1

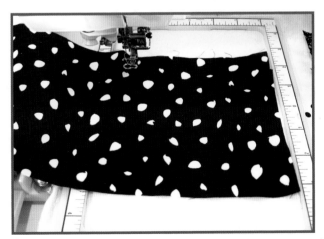

Stitch Large Blocks, Figure 2

Stitch color 2 (Figure 3). Without removing the hoop from the machine, trim inside the curve (Figure 4). Place a 4" piece of light fabric on the inside left corner, covering the smaller curve (Figure 5). Stitch color 3. Without removing the hoop from the machine, trim outside the curve (Figure 6).

Place a 5" square of black fabric over the center curve. Stitch color 4 (Figure 7). Lift the top frame of the hoop and slide the fabric up, leaving at least 1" between the blocks. Repeat these steps for the remaining blocks, substituting the appropriate colors for the other color schemes.

Stitch Large Blocks, Figure 3

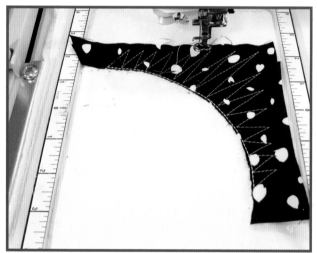

Stitch Large Blocks, Figure 4

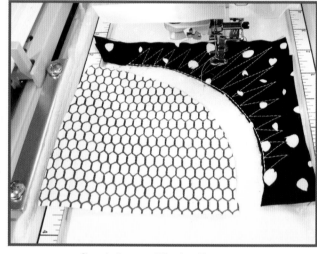

Stitch Large Blocks, Figure 5

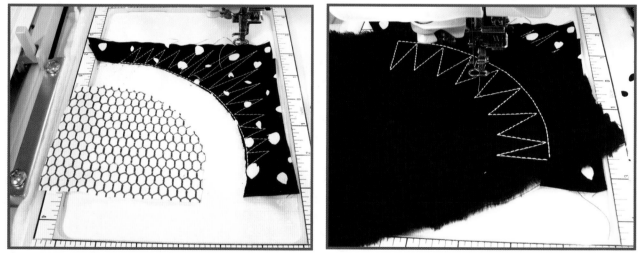

Stitch Large Blocks, Figure 6

Stitch Large Blocks, Figure 7

CREATE THE SETTING STONES

Hoop a 9" × 18" piece of pink fabric along with batting and backing. Stitch ten NY Setting Stone designs, all spaced at least 1" apart. Hoop a 9" × 10" piece of aqua fabric with batting and backing, and stitch six NY Setting Stone designs, all spaced at least 1" apart.

MAKE THE BLACK OUTER BORDER

Cut six 9" × WOF strips of black fabric, batting and backing. Hoop one end of the quilt sandwich and stitch the NY BeautyStipple design. Move the fabric up and stitch another square stipple block at least 1" away from the first. Repeat these steps to create thirty-six square stipple blocks.

PREPARE THE PIECES FOR ASSEMBLY

Trim all black-and-white blocks to 6" square. Trim all excess appliqué fabrics, leaving the inner and outer corner fabrics to extend into the block's seam allowance. This eliminates the chance of the white base fabric peeking through at the seams. Trim the square stipple blocks to 6" square and the setting stones to 3" square.

ASSEMBLE THE FOUR-BLOCK UNITS

Separate the blocks into darks and lights. Arrange the blocks into groups of four. Examine each unit and make sure the fabrics are varied. Avoid creating units with the same fabrics in each outer corner because these fabrics are the most visible. Keep the four-block units grouped together so you can piece the units at your leisure. You might find it helpful to place each unit in a plastic sandwich bag or pin the blocks together to avoid confusion later on.

Stitch two blocks together using reversible piecing (see page 36–39) (Figure 1). Use 2" × 6" sashing strips cut from the leftover print fabrics for a finished sashing width of 1" with ½" seam allowances. Stitch two pairs of two-block units together using reversible piecing to form a four-block unit (Figure 2). Stitch five dark units and four light units.

PIECE THE HALF UNITS

Piece the remaining blocks into two-block units for the perimeter of the quilt. You will need four dark and eight light half units. Using black sashing on the front, piece two black blocks to two half units (Figure 1).

Piece each of the four remaining dark blocks to three black blocks. Reserve for the corners.

Assemble the Four-Block Units, Figure 1

Assemble the Four-Block Units, Figure 2

Piece the Half Units, Figure 1

113

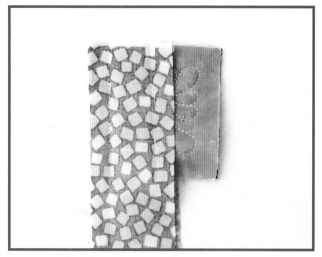

Stitch the Units Together, Figure 1

Stitch the Units Together, Figure 2

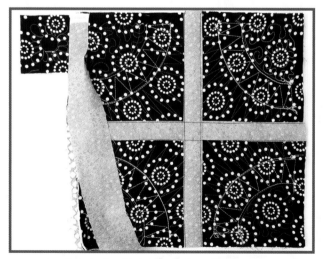

Stitch the Units Together, Figure 3

STITCH THE UNITS TOGETHER

Cut the remaining twenty-four front and back sashing strips to 2" × 15". Sew a front and back sashing strip to one side of a setting stone (Figure 1). Stop stitching ½" from the lower edge of the setting stone. Press the front sashing open. Sew the front sashing only to a four-block unit (Figure 2). Press the sashing from the front.

Flip the unit over, fold the back sashing over and press under a ½" seam allowance on the back sashing. Pin the back sashing in place (Figure 3). Edgestitch on the front along the sashing to catch the fold on the back. Edgestitch just ¾" and stop.

Add front and back sashing strips to the top of the unit (Figure 4). Set aside. Repeat for the remaining eight four-block units.

Now, piece the units together, using reversible piecing, alternating dark and light units (Figure 5). Refer to the photo of the finished quilt for guidance in placing the blocks. I found it was best to stop sewing both front and back sashings ½" from all edges. This left more options to add the next unit and it cut down on unnecessary ripping.

Add the outer blocks, keeping the black portions on the outside edge (Figure 6). Square off the quilt with a quilter's ruler.

Bind the quilt using a traditional method or the super-fast, fusible binding method (see page 40). The 1"-wide binding on this quilt adds a bit more punch than a standard ½" binding. Cut the binding strips 2" wide to show a 1"-wide finished binding. Add a sleeve and label to the back of the quilt if you desire.

Stitch the Units Together, Figure 4

Stitch the Units Together, Figure 5

Stitch the Units Together, Figure 6

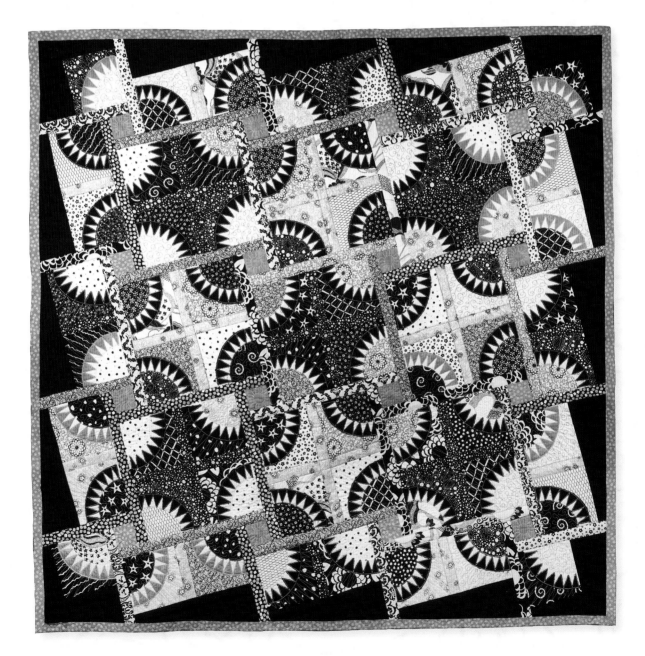

Basket of Blooms

FINISHED SIZE: 21¾" × 21¾"

This project uses the following files: FlorAp TopF1, FlorApBlock2F1, FlorApBottomBasketF1, FlorApBottomF1, FlorApCornerF1, FlorApMiddleF2, FlorApTopBasketF1

Basket of Blooms is a sweet wall hanging. In my main version, I had some fun with plaid fabrics, black-and-white dots and colorful batiks, but it would look luscious stitched on black with jewel tone appliqués, as you'll see in the figures below and on the following pages.

I also chose a fabric that reminded me of a basket for the bottom portion of the design, but a blue-and-white print would give the appearance of a vase. There are lots of possibilities in these designs! Choose your own fabrics to create a unique look.

Make sure you follow the order of the stitching for both the border and basket block. Some appliqués are camouflaging elements of other appliqués that are stitched first. Read through the instructions before embarking on this project.

MAKE THE HORIZONTAL AND VERTICAL BORDERS

Make one 15" × 20" quilt sandwich of base fabric, batting and backing fabric. Place the 1" mark of a quilter's ruler on the left long side of the quilt sandwich. Place a strip of painter's tape on the fabric along the edge of the ruler. Use the painter's tape as a guide when hooping the quilt sandwich (Figure 1). To conserve fabric, both borders will be stitched on this quilt sandwich with at least 1½" between the two borders.

Each border is made of three designs—FlorAp TopF1, FlorApMiddleF2 and FlorApBottomF1. The designs will not only connect, but they will actually overlap to make the continuous border. The middle design, FlorApMiddleF2, is stitched first, then the top and bottom designs to camouflage the overlapping points.

To stitch the FlorApMiddleF2 design, find and hoop the horizontal center of the quilt sandwich with the edge of the painter's tape just barely in the left side of the hoop. Make sure the tape is not in the sewing field since it is only there as a vertical guide. Stitch colors 1, the alignment marks, and 2, the stipple (Figure 2).

GATHER THESE ITEMS

Base fabric: ¾ yd.

Appliqué fabrics:

    one fat quarter of green fabric

    one fat quarter of aqua fabric

    one fat eighth of yellow fabric

    assorted fabric scraps for flowers

Backing fabric: ¾ yd.

Batting: 28" × 45"

5" × 7" hoop

NOTES FROM NANCY

Eileen has referenced painter's tape throughout the book. It's amazing how household supplies can transition to embroidery notions! Since learning this new use of painter's tape, I keep a roll next to my embroidery machine.

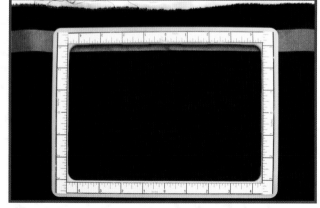

Make the Horizontal and Vertical Borders, Figure 1

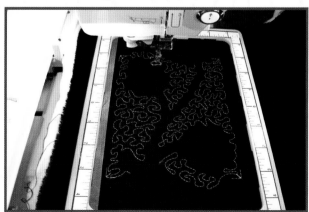

Make the Horizontal and Vertical Borders, Figure 2

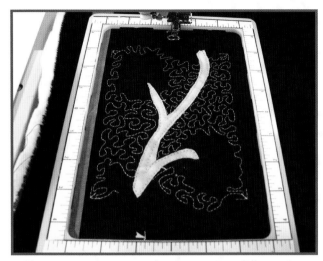
Make the Horizontal and Vertical Borders, Figure 3

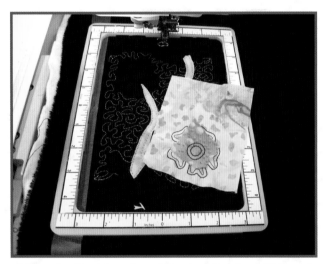
Make the Horizontal and Vertical Borders, Figure 4

After color 2 is complete, place green appliqué fabric over the open stem area. Stitch color 3, the stem tackdown. Carefully remove the hoop from the machine and trim the excess stem fabric (Figure 3).

Reattach the hoop to the machine. Place a square of flower appliqué fabric over the open area in the lower right corner of the hoop. Stitch colors 4 and 5. Place a small square of appliqué fabric over the flower center and stitch color 6 (Figure 4).

Place a square of flower appliqué fabric over the open area in the upper left corner of the hoop. Stitch colors 7 and 8. Place a small square of appliqué fabric over the flower center and stitch color 9 (Figure 5).

To move on to the top design, FlorAp TopF1, lift the hoop's top frame and slide the fabric down. Make sure the alignment marks from the middle design are within the sewing field in the new area. Use the painter's tape to square the fabric in the hoop.

To make the continuous border, the designs will not only connect, but they will overlap. Move the top design so the alignment marks touch. If your machine only allows movement of the design before a stitch is taken, move the design in the general direction of the previously stitched design. Advance one stitch. Note the location of the needle. If it is touching the previously stitched alignment mark, then proceed with the design (Figure 6). If not, go back to the beginning of the design and move to the proper location. This may take a few attempts, but it's well worth the effort because the stippling stitches and appliqués will link seamlessly with this method.

Make the Horizontal and Vertical Borders, Figure 5

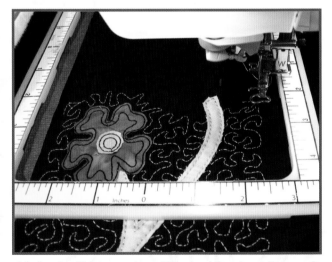
Make the Horizontal and Vertical Borders, Figure 6

Stitch colors 1 and 2 of the top design, the alignment marks and stipple stitches. Place a piece of flower appliqué fabric over the opening and stitch color 3, the appliqué tackdown. When color 3 is complete, place a small piece of appliqué fabric over the flower center area. Stitch color 4 (Figure 7).

Lift the top of the hoop and reposition the fabric to frame the bottom of the quilt sandwich. Use the painter's tape as an alignment guide. Move the bottom design so the alignment marks touch as they did when you joined the top and middle designs (Figure 8). Stitch FlorApBottomF1 starting with colors 1 and 2, the alignment marks and stipple stitches (Figure 9).

Place a piece of green appliqué fabric over the vine area and stitch color 3, the vine and leaf tackdown. Carefully remove the hoop from the machine and trim the excess vine fabric. Place appliqué fabric over the flower area and stitch color 4, the flower tackdown. Place a small piece of appliqué fabric over the flower center and stitch color 5, the center tackdown (Figure 10).

Remove the fabric from the hoop. Reposition the painter's tape, leaving at least 1½" between the first border and the second. Repeat all steps for the second border.

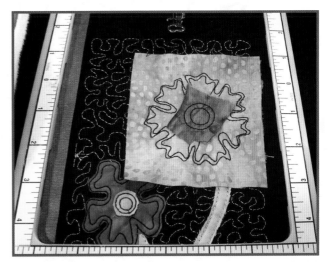

Make the Horizontal and Vertical Borders, Figure 7

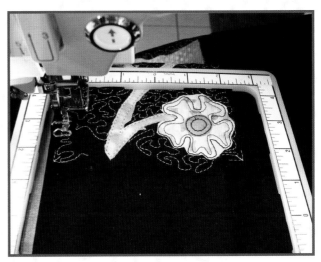

Make the Horizontal and Vertical Borders, Figure 8

Make the Horizontal and Vertical Borders, Figure 9

Make the Horizontal and Vertical Borders, Figure 10

STITCH THE BASKET OF BLOOMS

Make a 20" square quilt sandwich. Fold and press the fabric in half and in half again. Draw a 15" square on the center of the fabric.

Place the quilt sandwich on a flat surface and position the FlorApTopBasketF1 and FlorApBottom BasketF1 templates on the center of the block. Place the basket's upper edge over the stems of the flowers.

Place one FlorApCornerF1 template at each corner (Figure 1). Use a quilter's ruler to make sure all of the FlorApCornerF1 designs are square and parallel to each other. Check that the basket and flowers are centered. Once you're satisfied with the arrangement, slide target stickers under each template.

Hoop the quilt sandwich, centering the FlorAp TopBasketF1 target sticker. Place a piece of green appliqué fabric over the hooped area. Stitch color 1, the tackdown of all stems.

After completing color 1, carefully remove the hoop from the machine and trim the excess appliqué fabric. Don't trim the lower portions of the stems; they will come in handy when adding the basket in the second hooping.

Reattach the hoop to the machine (Figure 2). Stitch color 2, a placement guide for the small dot flowers. After completing color 2, place appliqué fabrics over the outlines and stitch color 3, the tackdown (Figure 3).

Carefully remove the hoop from the machine and trim the excess appliqué fabric. Detailed trimming can be done later when the fabric is removed from the hoop. Reattach the hoop to the machine. Place a piece of appliqué fabric at the top right of the hoop. Use your template as a reference for fabric placement. Stitch color 4, the flower tackdown (Figure 4).

Stitch the Basket of Blooms, Figure 1

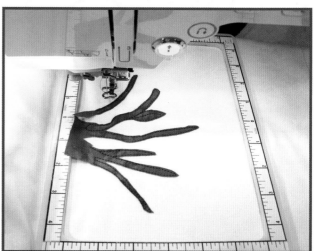

Stitch the Basket of Blooms, Figure 2

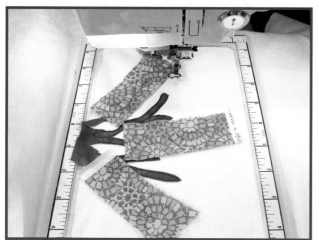

Stitch the Basket of Blooms, Figure 3

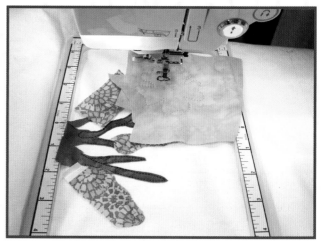

Stitch the Basket of Blooms, Figure 4

Place a piece of contrasting appliqué fabric over the center of the flower and stitch color 5, the inner flower tackdown. Place a small piece of contrasting appliqué fabric over the center of the flower and stitch color 6, the flower center tackdown (Figure 5).

Place a piece of appliqué fabric at the bottom right of the hoop. Again, use your template as a reference if necessary. Stitch color 7, the tackdown. Place a piece of appliqué fabric over the flower and stitch color 8, the tackdown. Place a piece of print fabric over the flower center and stitch color 9, the tackdown (Figure 6).

Remove the fabric from the hoop and place it on a flat surface. Notice the target sticker is still in position for the FlorApBottomBasketF1 design. Place the FlorApBottomBasketF1 template on the target sticker. Align the template and target sticker crosshairs (Figure 7). Analyze the placement. If the upper edge of the basket is not covering the bottom of the stems, move the template and realign the target sticker.

Hoop the fabric, centering the FlorApBottom BasketF1 target sticker. Position the needle over the target sticker and remove the sticker. Stitch color 1, the placement guide for the basket. The outline will verify that the ends of the stems will be covered by the basket.

Place a piece of green appliqué fabric over the top of the basket; use the template as a reference for placement. Stitch color 2, the tackdown of the stems (Figure 8). Carefully remove the hoop from the machine and trim the excess stem fabric. Reattach the hoop to the machine.

Stitch the Basket of Blooms, Figure 5

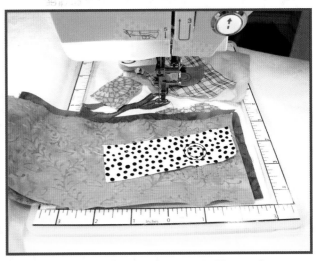

Stitch the Basket of Blooms, Figure 6

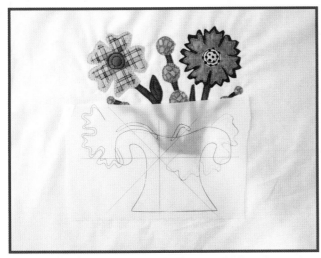

Stitch the Basket of Blooms, Figure 7

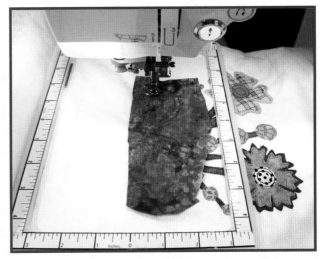

Stitch the Basket of Blooms, Figure 8

Lay the basket appliqué fabric over the basket outline. Stitch colors 3, the tackdown, and 4, the basket grid. Remove the hoop from the machine and trim the basket appliqué. Reattach the hoop to the machine.

Refer to the template and place appliqué fabric at the tip of the stem at the top of the hoop. Stitch color 5, the flower tackdown. Place appliqué fabric at the tip of the stem at the bottom of the hoop. Stitch color 6, the flower tackdown. Place a second piece of appliqué fabric in the same area and stitch color 7, the inner flower tackdown. Place a piece of green appliqué fabric at the stem of the flower and stitch color 8, the tackdown (Figure 9).

Color 9 is the detail of the first flower located at the top of the hoop. You could add an additional layer of appliqué here if desired. Stitch color 9. Place a piece of green fabric over the flower and stitch color 10, the stem tackdown.

Take the fabric out of the hoop and place it on a flat surface. Position the FlorApCornerF1 templates at each corner and double-check their placement (Figure 10). Hoop one corner. Lay a 5" square of appliqué fabric over the hoop. Stitch colors 1, 2 and 3, the tackdown and details.

Switch your thread and place appliqué fabric over the circles in the design and stitch color 4 (Figure 11). Repeat for each corner.

STITCH THE SETTING BLOCK

Hoop an 8" × 10" quilt sandwich. Stitch FlorAp Block2F1 starting with color 1, the grid. Place a 6" square of appliqué fabric over the block and stitch color 2, the tackdown, and color 3, the outline of the dots. Place appliqué fabric over each dot and stitch color 4, the dot tackdown (Figure 1).

Stitch the Basket of Blooms, Figure 9

Stitch the Basket of Blooms, Figure 10

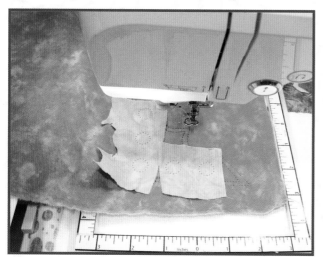

Stitch the Basket of Blooms, Figure 11

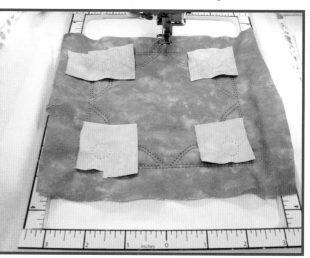

Stitch the Setting Block, Figure 1

TRIM AND PIECE THE DESIGNS

Use a quilter's ruler to trim all quilt sandwiches. Place the ruler's ½" mark on the edge of the embroidery and trim away the excess fabric and batting.

Cut a 2" × 6" front and back sashing strip. Use these sashing strips, reversible piecing and ½" seam allowances to piece the horizontal border to the setting block (see pages 36–39). Cut a 2" × 15½" front and back sashing strip. Piece the basket block to the vertical border using these sashing strips and reversible piecing. Cut a 2" × 21½" front and back sashing strip. Add these horizontal sashing strips to the lower edge of the basket unit. Piece the lower border unit to the basket unit.

Bind the quilt using a traditional method or the super-fast, fusible binding method (see page 40). Add a sleeve and label to the back of the quilt if you desire.

123

Embroidery Designs

Raggedy Edge Coasters
CoasterF1

No-Sew Pin Cushion
Heart Cushion AppF3

Plume Pillow
*PlumeCtrF1
(above),
Plume2F1 (left)*

Pieced Pin Cushion
*Left to Right:
Heart Pin CushionF1,
Heart Pin Cushion BackF1,
HeartPatchF1*

Trapunto Table
Runner
*Left to Right: Fleur
De Lis CenterF1,
Fleur de lisF1,
CornerF1*

My Favorite Bag
*Top Row, Left to Right: Swirl TopF1, Swirl BottomF1;
Bottom Row, Left to Right: CircleGrommetF1, Cool
FlowerF2, DiamondNarrowBorderF2*

Scallop Tote
*Grid oneLineF1 (bottom),
ContScallopCircF1 (top)*

Sewing Notions Caddy
*Diamond GridF2 (bottom), Floral
SwagF2 (top)*

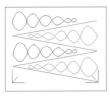

Ohio Star Quilt
Top Row, Left to Right: OhStDiamondBlkF1, OhioStarNoSqF1;
Bottom Row, Left to Right: Ohio BorderF1, Ohio Star CornerF1

Basket of Blooms
Top Row (at left): FlorAp TopF1;
Second Row, Left to Right:
FlorApMiddleF2, FlorApTopBasketF1,
FlorApBlock2F1, FlorApCornerF1;
Bottom Row, Left to Right: FlorAp
BottomF1, FlorApBottomBasketF1

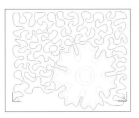

Lady Liberty Quilt
Left Column, top to bottom: LLMidBorderF2 LadyLiber-
tyL6F2, LL3 DiamondF1; Right Column, top to bottom:
LLCorner2F2, LLBorder6F1, LLBorder2F1

New York Beauty Quilt
NY Setting Stone (left), NY Beauty
(bottom left), NY BeautyStipple
(bottom right)

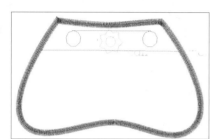

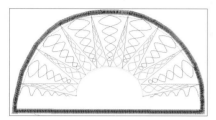

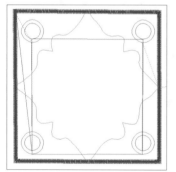

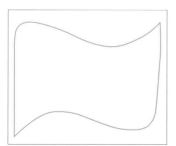

Resources

EMBROIDERY TOOLS

Designs in Machine Embroidery
www.dzgns.com
800-739-0555
Magna-Hoop, Snap-Hoop, target stickers, target rulers, Angle Finder and the Embroidery Tool Kit

BATTING

The Warm Company
www.warmcompany.com
425-248-2424

THREAD

Sulky
www.sulky.com
800-874-4115

YLI
www.ylicorp.com
803-985-3100

American & Efird
www.amefird.com
704-827-4311

DIGITIZING SERVICES

NetEmb
www.netemb.com
800-998-3334

FURTHER READING

Designs in Machine Embroidery magazine
www.dzgns.com

OTHER BOOKS BY EILEEN ROCHE FROM KRAUSE PUBLICATIONS

Contemporary Machine Embroidered Accessories
Contemporary Machine-Embroidered Fashions
Contemporary Machine Embroidered Quilts

AUTHOR'S BLOG

eileenroche.wordpress.com

Index

Stitch to your heart's content

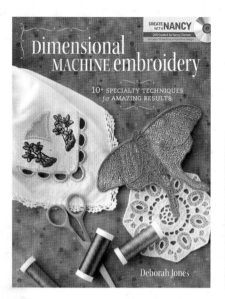

Dimensional Machine Embroidery

10+ Specialty Techniques for Amazing Results

Deborah Jones

Learn 11 unique specialty techniques that will expand your machine embroidery options. Ten specific projects demonstrate the techniques and their versatility. The book includes helpful hints from Nancy Zieman that will give you the insight and confidence to try new things. The accompanying how-to DVD will give you a visual step-by-step introduction to taking your basic machine embroidery to new heights.

paperback; 8.25" × 10.875"; 112 pages
ISBN-10: 1-4402-0397-0
ISBN-13: 978-1-4402-0397-8
SRN: Z2050

Piece in the Hoop

20 Quilt Patterns + 40 Machine Embroidered Designs

Larisa Bland

Forty embroidery and quilt block designs and 20 projects for using stitchout blocks demonstrate Piece in the Hoop—a technique where quilters sew precise quilt blocks on an embroidery machine. This book includes helpful hints from Nancy Zieman and a helpful how-to DVD.

paperback; 8.25" × 10.75"; 128 pages
ISBN-10: 1-4402-0356-3
ISBN-13: 978-1-4402-0356-5
SRN: Z4957

Patchwork & Stitchery

12 Quilt Projects with Embroidered Twists

Carol Phillipson

Patchwork & Stitchery combines the joys of traditional pieced and appliqué quiltmaking and the art of stitchery (embroidery, redwork, mixed stitches, sashiko and cross-stitch) to create an individualized quilt. The book includes basic techniques for quilting, appliqué and stitches, as well as 12 quilt projects, each with different colorwaves and planning techniques (including designing on computer). The CD with the book features 100 stitched designs.

paperback; 8.25" × 10.875"; 128 pages
ISBN-10: 1-4402-0235-4
ISBN-13: 978-1-4402-0235-3
SRN: Z4957